An Outline of Psychotherapy
for Trainee Psychiatrists,
Medical Students and
Practitioners
2nd edition

To M (C)
With love

An Outline of Psychotherapy for Trainee Psychiatrists, Medical Students and Practitioners

2nd edition

Edited by

HAROLD MAXWELL, MD, FRCPsych

Consultant Psychotherapist and Honorary Senior Lecturer
West Middlesex Hospital and Charing Cross and Westminster Medical School
Member of the British Psychoanalytical Society

With a Foreword by

STEPHEN R. HIRSCH, BA, MD, MPhil, FRCP, FRCPsych

Professsor of Psychiatry
Charing Cross and Westminster Medical School
University of London

W

Whurr Publishers Ltd
London and New Jersey

© Whurr Publishers Limited 1990, 1991

First published 1986 by IOP Publishing Limited
Republished 1990 by Whurr Publishers Ltd
Second edition published by Whurr Publishers Ltd
19b Compton Terrace, London N1 2UN

Reprinted 1993 and 1997

British Library Cataloguing-in-Publication Data
An outline of psychotherapy for trainee
psychiatrists and medical students. – 2nd ed.
  I. Maxwell, Harold
  616.89

  ISBN 1-870332-62-8

Phototypeset by J&L Composition Ltd, Filey, North Yorkshire
Printed in Great Britain by Athenæum Press Ltd, Gateshead, Tyne & Wear

Foreword

STEVEN HIRSCH

This book is suitable for anyone who wants to have a broad introduction to the psychotherapies. Medical students generally enjoy their period as a student in psychiatry, though they do not expect to do so. Most doctors going through medical school only a half generation before had less exposure to the specialty. For both generations, the word psychotherapy remains one they have heard of and, nowadays, they may have experienced the subject transiently as a member of a seminar group, but this is rarely satisfactory. As teachers of psychiatry, we continue to be asked by students and trainee psychiatrists for something about psychotherapy which is didactic and direct – something which can be written down, thought about and studied. But chapters in text books are too short to convey the breadth, depth and relevance of the approach, and books written for the committed tend to be too narrow or too ambitious. For an answer to the questions. 'What is psychotherapy?', 'How does it work?', 'What does it consist of?', this little book gets it about right. It is not too long to read in one or two evenings, or too detailed to lose the reader's interest. It covers the field broadly from psychoanalytically based therapy to family systems theory and conditioning-based behaviour therapy. The main psychoanalytical concepts are nicely summarised and clearly defined and there is an insightful chapter on what happens to the medical student's feelings as a novice actor in the arena of acute medicine. The possibility for the physician in general practice or any specialty to make use of a psychotherapeutic sixth sense which will help in the management of his patients is explored in a chapter on liaison psychiatry, and in another on general practice. This is a very down-to-earth and practical book which should be useful for anyone who wants to know something of how psychotherapy works and what it has to offer. It will be relevant to those outside the medical profession and in related fields, such as social work, as well as for those within.

It is not, of course, a matter of chance that this book appears at this time. While general psychiatry was maturing and developing clinical and scientific

credibility, it had little time for this area of endeavour which is not necessarily medical, and in which scientific hypotheses which test research are still
scant. The lack of such reason is the fault of its devotees who, for too long,
have clung to early concepts that have heuristic value, but need translation
into verifiable operational concepts which can be recognised as right or
wrong. One problem has been the unwillingness of psychotherapists and
analysts to test the effectiveness of their treatment by criteria which
lie outside their field of theoretical discourse, such as return to work,
resumption of sexual activity, lessening of anxiety and depression scores,
lower relapse rates or, in the case of liaison psychiatry, improvement in the
patients' physical functioning. Yet, recent studies have begun to show that
psychotherapy is a powerful technique by these criteria. Another reason for
the dearth of research is that practitioners are, rightfully to some extent,
convinced by their own experience – because they almost all undergo therapy
as a requisite to training. The training is long, arduous and expensive and the
commitment of most therapists once trained is to their patients and to the
exercise of their long-won skills; they experience research as antithetical to
all this. Fortunately, there is a small but growing number of psychotherapy
research workers who are beginning to demonstrate the efficacy of
psychotherapy and earn its respect as a bona fide treatment within medicine.

This book is timely because we are now witnessing an exploding interest in
psychotherapy on the part of the public and a growing appreciation by the
medical profession at all levels of what it has to offer. This may reflect an
increasing standard of living for those in society who expect more for
themselves and are less willing to tolerate inner turmoil and difficulties in
their relationships with others.

Although our own Department of Psychiatry at Charing Cross is biologically oriented in research, and community-oriented from a service point
of view, we require all our psychiatrists in training to obtain experience in
psychotherapy, because we believe the skills are essential if someone wants to
address him- or herself fully to a patient's treatment. This concern is also
reflected in recent changes in the membership examinations of the Royal
College of Psychiatry. Similarly, our trainee psychiatrists are all being given
an opportunity to treat a patient psychotherapeutically, if they wish, and
there is now a liaison psychiatry and psychotherapy service throughout our
hospital which is appreciated by physicians, surgeons and obstetricians alike.

The growing demand by the public for 'humanistic medicine' and the
increasing interest in fringe medicine of all sorts is further evidence of this
new ethic. If doctors can guard against the erosion of that sensitivity and
human interest they had before they even entered an anatomy room, and go
on to develop the skills which will enable them to use these qualities as they
carry out their medical work, the demand for fringe medicine will be kept at
bay. This primer is a very good starting point for such a task.

Preface to the 2nd edition

This book was originally compiled for medical students and family doctors, and gained inclusion in the Royal College of Psychiatrists' 'List of books suitable for a psychiatric library 1983–87'.

With reconstructions and additional material, *trainee psychiatrists* can now also look to its pages for a background of psychotherapy theory and practice. Indeed, it is hoped that all doctors engaged in clinical work will find its present format and content of use.

As outlined in the preface of the first edition, recent years have seen the continued humanisation of medical practice. The policy is exemplified in the undergraduate curriculum which now includes, in most medical schools, at least some elements of the fostering of empathy with the patient, as opposed to the mere inculcation of scientific detached attitudes. A greater self-awareness among doctors themselves is also now acceptable and even encouraged, and in this regard Jon Sklar's chapter has been considerably and sympathetically expanded. Psychiatric and personality casualties within the medical profession, at all ages, are issues about which the profession itself is becoming increasingly aware.

In the psychotherapeutic armamentarium, *cognitive methods* have an established place, as outlined in a new chapter by David Clark. Alan Cooklin's account of work with families now includes a consideration of ethnic factors, whilst 'liaison psychiatry' is presented in a more complete form.

David Alexander's introductory chapter, itself augmented, receives an editorial boost with a look at some notes on psychoanalysis since Freud.

Again, there are many people to thank for their help in compiling the volume, and I particularly include Dr C.A. Vassilas of Bristol, Dr Frances Raphael and Dr Phil Mollon.

Special thanks are extended by the editor and Whurr Publishers to Messrs Churchill-Livingstone for permission to reproduce part of Dr Hale's chapter from the forthcoming book, *Psychotherapy in Psychiatric Practice* (1991).

Harold Maxwell
London, 1991

Preface to the 1st edition

If then our judgment be so depraved, our reason overruled, (our) will precipitated, that we cannot seek our own good, or moderate ourselves, as to melancholia commonly it is, the best way for ease is to impart our misery to some friend, not to smother it up in our own breast; for grief concealed strangles the soul, but when as we shall impart it to some discreet trusty loving friend, it is instantly removed, for a friend's counsel is a charm; like mandrake wine it allayeth all our cares.

'The Anatomie of Melancholie',
1621, by Robert Burton

I make no apology for putting together in one volume an assemblage of my own main professional interests: psychoanalysis, psychotherapy and liaison medicine.

Psychotherapy is about people and their feelings. There is no line separating patients, doctors and medical students. At the same time, while not everyone becomes, say, a bronchitic or a diabetic, or has a baby, everyone will at various times experience grief, sadness, elation, envy, fear, paranoia, sleep disturbances, rage and muddled thoughts concerning the problems of living and relating; all these constitute the very stuff of psychiatry and also of this book. Incidentally, it would not have found a market within the world of the medical establishment when I qualified in 1950. Today's mores are, however, thankfully different, being exemplified by the remark of a young male trainee general practitioner who said in a recent seminar. 'Of course in certain circumstances I would feel it natural to hold the hand of, or even put my arm around, a patient, male or female, if in doing so I felt that it would comfort them ...'. The other members of the seminar agreed.

The book was designed with all clinicians in mind, but medical students and other beginners may find it particularly helpful to refer initially to Chapters 1 and 3 as a basis.

It is a pleasure to acknowledge my thanks to the contributors to this book, also to the publishers, and to Aberdeen University Press for allowing

Dr Alexander's chapter to appear, the latter being an extended version of that published in *Models for Psychotherapy* by J.D.H. Haldane, D.A. Alexander and L.G.W. Walker. My wife Marianne kindly read the proofs and made many helpful suggestions.

HM
London, December 1985

Contributors

David Alexander, PhD, Senior Lecturer in Mental Health, University of Aberdeen

Dick Blackwell, BSc, Member of the Institute of Group Analysis

David M. Clark, DPhil, Lecturer in Psychology, University Department of Psychiatry, Warneford Hospital, Oxford

Alan Cooklin, MB, ChB, FRCPsych, Consultant Family Psychiatrist, Marlborough Day Hospital, London

Andrew Elder, MB, BS, MRCGP, General Practitioner, London

Robert Hale, FRCPsych, Consultant Psychotherapist, The Tavistock Clinic, London
Associate Member, British Psychoanalytical Society

Alan King, BSc MB, ChB, MRCPsych, Consultant Behavioural Psycho-therapist, Leicester Royal Infirmary

Harold Maxwell, MD, FRCPsych, Consultant Psychotherapist and Honorary Senior Lecturer, West Middlesex Hospital, and Charing Cross and Westminster Medical School, London
Member, British Psychoanalytical Society

Jon Sklar, MB, BS, MRCPsych, Consultant Psychotherapist, Addenbroke's Hospital, Cambridge
Member, British Psychoanalytical Society

Chris Thomas, MB, BS, MRCP, MRCPsych, Consultant Liaison Psychiatrist, County Hospital, Hereford

Contents

Foreword   v

Preface to 2nd edition   vii

Preface to 1st edition   viii

Contributors   x

Chapter 1

Psychotherapy: A general introduction, *Harold Maxwell*   1

Chapter 2

Psychodynamic therapy, *David Alexander*   12

Chapter 3

Departures from the traditional Freudian way, *Harold Maxwell*   40

Chapter 4

The trainee's feelings and the clinical relationship, *Jon Sklar*   48

Chapter 5

Psychotherapy in liaison psychiatry, *Chris Thomas*   55
Addendum I: Liaison psychiatry and parasuicide – a bridge,
Harold Maxwell   70
Addendum II: Psychotherapy in the management of
attempted suicide, *Robert Hale*   71

Chapter 6

Psychotherapy in general practice, *Andrew Elder*   **74**

Chapter 7

Group psychotherapy, *Dick Blackwell*   **92**

Chapter 8

Therapy, the family and others, *Alan Cooklin*   **105**

Chapter 9

Behaviour therapy, *Alan King*   **129**

Chapter 10

Cognitive therapy, *David Clark*   **142**

Further general reading   **149**

Index   **151**

Chapter 1
Psychotherapy: A General Introduction

HAROLD MAXWELL

The content of this volume pertains to psychotherapy by *medical personnel*, including students. It is necessary, however, to note that, unlike medicine, psychotherapy per se is a completely unregistered profession and consequently there is no body such as the General Medical Council responsible for the activities of psychotherapists. Certain members of several core professions, e.g. psychiatry, psychology, nursing and social work, all practise psychotherapy and when doing so are answerable to their own professional bodies. There are, however, other psychotherapists who have trained in various ways, and may not necessarily have a background in one of the caring professions. Some of these people will belong to professional organisations such as the British Psychoanalytical Society, the Society for Analytical Psychology and the British Association of Psychotherapists, although anyone can in fact call him- or herself a 'psychotherapist' or even a 'psychoanalyst'.

Nevertheless, a significant number of people seeking help by psychotherapy will turn to members of the medical profession, which still enjoys a remarkable degree of trust on the part of the general public. Medical personnel who are psychotherapists will usually have been trained as general psychiatrists and in addition will have followed courses leading to membership of one of the three bodies referred to above. As far as other medical personnel are concerned, to some extent it will be the degree of *involvement* with the patient, both in intensity and duration, which will affect the 'depth' of the physician's influence. Those with minimum involvement would naturally include, say, clinical pathologists and radiologists, while at the other end of the spectrum would be the family doctor with his or her 'permanent' relationship and the general psychiatrist. In between would be every specialist category pertaining to clinical work.

Nowadays, there seems to be a greater emphasis placed on what has come to be called the doctor–patient relationship in general medicine and surgery, dermatology, obstetrics and, especially, gynaecology. The *family practitioner's* use of psychotherapy is covered elsewhere (Chapter 6), whilst the *general psychiatrist* will involve him- or herself in supportive and insight-directed psychotherapy, to an extent that varies with his or her own inclinations, in this way supplementing his physical and social measures in the total management of patients.

In the sphere of both general and psychiatric practice the teaching of *Michael Balint*, which is also discussed elsewhere, will be remembered with its credo of the doctor–patient relationship. Naturally, this factor had been known long before Balint described it, but was never so well delineated in practical terms. However, a remarkable paper by Houston (1939) just before the Second World War, emphasised the placebo effect of the doctor him- or herself as a therapeutic agent. The point was made that throughout history the number of pharmacological preparations with a 'genuine' and predictable action was extremely small and the 'greatness' of physicians, effectively up to the nineteenth or even twentieth century, depended upon the *personality* of that physician and its placebo effect (i.e. the faith evoked in the efficacy of the doctor's personality). Hypnosis and other modern 'popular' procedures with no physiological validation are based on the same mechanism.

Principles of Individual Therapy

What is psychotherapy?

Psychotherapy is a professional way of dealing with human misery and unhappiness, including psychiatric states, by the interaction of the patient with one or more people. It can be individual, group, marital or family. The most usual method of interaction is through talk and the psychotherapy which ensues may, as already noted, be supportive or insightful, the latter hopefully leading to development of the personality. Psychotherapy in the context of this book is concerned with clinical practice: it may or may not be used in combination with physical methods of treatment such as drugs.

Where?

The setting is extremely important. Its degree of opulence does not matter, its *constancy* does. Usually a small- or medium-sized room, quietly furnished with the absence of distractions of, say, the telephone, with both the patient and therapist being physically comfortable, is adequate.

Who?

The psychotherapist is a professional – for our purposes a physician. He or she will have had at least some training, may belong to one of the so-called 'schools' of psychotherapy and will probably have had some personal therapy or analysis.

Features of Psychotherapy

Generally, psychotherapy will be either *supportive*, i.e. 'encouraging the positive', or will hopefully enable the patient to gain *insight* into how and why factors from the past have determined his or her present predicament and how to a large extent he or she is compelled to repeat past patterns of inexpedient behaviour.

With the start of treatment, the patient will, by implication and at the very least, receive the message that he or she is 'worthy of help' and thereby experience enhancement to his or her self-esteem. The installation and maintenance of *hope* will also be a feature, which will be compounded by the constancy of the setting and of the therapist him- or herself. The latter cannot delegate this role to a locum or deputy: *psychotherapy is above all based on a human relationship.*

The initial interview

This is partly a fact-finding process but will differ from a medical model interview because, in addition to facts such as name, address, occupation etc., the patient's demeanour, dress and general attitudes will be noted. The overall mood which the patient evokes in the therapist is also important, especially in coming to an 'empathetic' diagnosis. The more adept and experienced the practitioner, the more accurate will be his or her antennae in receiving emotional messages from the patient.

The psychotherapy sessions

What takes place? Apart from implicit messages of support that are conveyed to the patient, *facilitation* is provided by the therapist by means of his or her interest, recognition and sense of receptiveness. *Confrontation* is also used as a means of making the patient aware of a reaction that has been provoked within the therapist. *Reassurance*, suggestion and direction are also employed, as is questioning, although the last should be used sparingly. *Interpretations* are a means of conveying to the patient an understanding on the part of the therapist, by which something implied or hidden from the patient's consciousness may be brought to his or her attention. Interpretations sometimes involve the therapist, when they are called transference interpretations, and as such are especially pertinent to orthodox psychoanalysis. *Advice* and *guidance* are also given, as well as reinforcement and behaviour modification. The last is conveyed to the patient by tacit approval, or otherwise, of the patient's activities, statements or decisions. *Silence* may be a problem to psychotherapists in training. It is of several kinds and the overriding mood will hopefully be picked up: hostile, neutral or restful. A therapeutic step forward during a silence would be for the therapist to say to the patient something like, 'I feel a bit lost and don't really know what to say' or 'I'm confused and rather muddled and I wonder whether you feel the same'. This will be a truism and will enable the patient to feel recognised and understood even if it is only in a 'negative' way, so that the basis may be laid for future, naturally more positive, experiences.

Supportive psychotherapy

This is the minimum type of psychotherapy. Evidence of good will, consistency and sincere interest is conveyed with an implicit promise that the patient, with all his or her fears, weaknesses, anxieties and above all his or her aggressiveness, will be received and contained by the therapist. As its name suggests, this psychotherapy is especially called for to support the patient during acute or long-standing periods of crisis. Clear-cut events such as bereavements or divorces may, for a given period of time, call for regular meetings with the patient so that the situations can be worked through and he or she may gradually come to terms with the situations. Those with a low threshold to life's exigencies may need, in the extreme, a life-long availability on the part of the therapist, who ideally will combine this role with that of family doctor. The very fact that the latter 'is there' may often be sufficient to prevent many patients breaking down. Good GPs have, in fact, had transferred to them aspects of a good parent, who will not condemn or judge, but will stay and be available. Non-medical counsellors are now being trained in considerable numbers to deal with the common-or-garden problems of living which many patients just cannot cope with and which in the past were dealt with by the priest, lawyer or lord of the manor.

Insight psychotherapy

This is a process whereby the patient is encouraged to understand that habitual 'defences' and methods of reacting to external situations may be inappropriate and unpropitious, often provoking other people. Hopefully, their origin in early life will be understood by both patient and therapist and conscious attempts at modification and change will be made. The use of dreams, slips of the tongue and ruminative free association of speech will be part of the process. Here the aim is more ambitious than in supportive psychotherapy. The patient will be helped to understand that certain patterns of responses to the environment are self-defeating, leading to further negative situations. This type of therapy is a way of showing a patient how he or she can, through reflection and given sufficient motivation, react with different patterns of behaviour. It is an experience based on psychoanalysis, and a certain amount of personal therapy for the doctor may be necessary in order to enable the therapist to distinguish between his or her own hang-ups and those of the patient.

It used to be thought by the early psychoanalysts that the aim of treatment was to 'make the unconscious, conscious'. Nowadays, we would hope that the degree of suffering by the individual may be reduced as a result of *integration*, i.e. the coming together and acceptance of various contradictory feelings and attitudes: that the 'pain' of these *ambivalences* will gradually lessen and become tolerable, so that maturing and positive processes will supervene, thus reducing the need for painful and costly defences to be employed with suffering for the person, the family or even society as a whole (see also Chapter 2).

Clinical Conditions where Psychotherapy may be considered

1. Supportive psychotherapy may be indicated when any of life's crises affecting the person or his or her family are being negotiated, e.g. divorce, redundancy, retirement, bereavement.
2. Psychiatric conditions, especially recurring states of baseless anxiety or depression; addictions; some of the schizophrenic illnesses.
3. 'Existential conditions' – probably the most common situations which the specialist, in particular, is nowadays called upon to treat. The symptomatology is vague, confused, alters from day to day and accounts for an ill-defined ennui whereby both isolation (loneliness) and its opposite – the too-invasive and too-close proximity of another person – are felt to be intolerable, so that an oscillation of depressive aloneness and suffocating relatedness is experienced, accounting for *difficulties in relationships*, sometimes with recourse to drugs and alcohol. Sexual problems of all types are included in this section.
4. Some medical states of an episodic or chronic nature, e.g. migraine; asthma; musculoskeletal diseases; and gastrointestinal symptoms

These conversion phenomena or psychosomatic conditions are usually very resistant to change by psychotherapy – frequently, they are best left to sympathetic management by the general physician or family doctor.

Factors to be considered in evaluation of the suitability for psychotherapy

Motivation

This will depend on the degree of real (mental) suffering or distress, usually anxiety and/or depression, and the determination to find a better *modus vivendi.*

Age

Age is not as important as might be imagined. Both the very young and the elderly can be helped.

'Ego strength'

This means the general cohesiveness and state of maturity of the personality, as shown by attainments in general, the sources of happiness, if any, and, above all, the ability or otherwise to *sustain* relationships both in personal life and in work situations.

Intelligence

A minimum is certainly necessary, but again this factor should not be over-emphasised. More important is the capacity or otherwise for insight and reflection, i.e. the presence of 'psychological-mindedness' (see below), and above all the *motivation* for change.

The ability to tolerate anxiety and frustration

This is important, because psychotherapy is often a slow process, not enjoying the instant relief that medication can often provide for symptoms. A history of 'acting out', i.e. the involvement of the patient in unpropitious or destructive activities, is a sign that psychotherapy may be especially difficult.

'Secondary gain'

This means, for instance, that by the maintenance of symptoms the patient may exercise considerable control over his or her environment, sometimes in a blackmailing way.

Reality factors

These include the availability of specialists, the willingness of the patient to invest time and sometimes money in his or her treatment and, ideally, a family situation which is objective towards psychotherapy.

Types of defences (see below)

If it seems that excessive denial, splitting, confusion or projection are employed, it will suggest that psychotherapy will be difficult, as would evidence of acting out (poor impulse control) or psychosomatic disease.

The discerning of 'psychological-mindedness' in the clinical interview

Coltart (1988) suggests some useful pointers, including evidence of 'imagination', the willingness to accept at least some responsibility for the events of one's own life, a record of minimal past successes or gratifications, and especially an 'overall impression' on the part of the observer, drawing on his or her own experience and empathetic constitution.

Psychoanalysis

This is a special method of psychotherapy invented by Freud, dealing particularly with transference. This special relationship which develops between a patient and the analyst is analysed and traced back to the patient's earliest relationships. Whilst most other forms of psychotherapy are based on suggestion and encouragement, psychoanalysis is concerned with the largely unconsciously derived and transferred feelings and attitudes with which the patients invests the analyst. This transference is to some extent fostered by the analyst, who remains relatively 'anonymous'.

Some psychoanalytical concepts

Defences

These are universal phenomena and must be respected. The 'defence' is against overwhelming *internal* anxiety, as opposed to 'real', or outside, physical dangers. It is important to grasp that there is an internal world as well as an external world and that the former does in fact determine many of our basic moods, responses, feelings, attitudes and, in a psychiatric sense, the types of *distortions* which may make human relationships difficult or even impossible. These distortions, especially towards other people, are based on attitudes to important figures from the past, often evoking difficulties which may never have been resolved, and perpetuating feelings which, even at the original time, may well have been inappropriate to the event taking place (*see* Transference).

It must be realised that it is only when these mechanisms become exaggerated or habitual, that they can be called pathological and, paradoxically, it is when they break down that psychiatric symptoms begin. Were it not for defence mechanisms, which automatically come into play when we meet with any unpleasant reality, life would soon become a severe burden, if not impossible. Such defences include the following.

Denial
This is a method whereby unpleasant events may conveniently be 'blotted out'. Examples would include the pain of recent bereavement, an unpleasant sight consequent upon an accident or other trauma, the usage of the 'sour grapes' phenomenon (i.e. something which has not, in reality, been available has its value denied). 'Splitting' is often associated with denial. It excludes life's grey areas: everything and everyone is black and white, good or bad etc.

Displacement
If hostile feelings or emotions cannot be expressed to authority or other powerful figures, they may be *displaced* on to others less threatening or further away; for instance, it is safe to hate an enemy on the other side of the world. Another example would be kicking the cat to release frustration towards someone whom you could not attack safely.

Phobic avoidance
Sometimes very primitive and deep-seated situations which evoke intolerable terror become focused on to specific objects or situations in the external world through a process of subtle and unconscious symbolic transformation. Thus, animals or other creatures, e.g. snakes and spiders, or situations such as open spaces or closed rooms, come to *stand for* these very primitive, sincerely 'forgotten' and very basic situations. The important point is how much of an inconvenience it is to avoid the substituted, external symbol of teror, e.g. it is not much of a problem for a snake-phobic living in a suburb of a big city, but a real fear of flying is, perhaps, a constraint for a businessman. (Chapter 9 will highlight these conditions and their management.)

Projection
This is ascribing to others negative feelings and attitudes in ourselves. It is the basis of paranoid states for, if we 'believe' that others are feeling or behaving badly, we are then justified in hating, hurting or attacking them in return.

Rationalisation
This is a means whereby the true reason for a course of action is hidden by *apparent* explanations.

Reaction formation
This denotes going to the opposite extreme towards experiences which may be morally unacceptable, e.g. excessive cleanliness to counteract innate wishes and instincts to be dirty, untruthful, inexact or spontaneous.

Regression
This denotes a return to a more child-like state, so that temporarily at least it is possible to re-experience being a child with no responsibilities. Naturally the phenomenon occurs in sleep and it is an acceptable event at times of illness when it is a sort of 'secondary gain'.

Repression and suppression
A way of putting off, or burying, painful or even exciting feelings or thoughts. As with all defence mechanisms, if it is too successful it is like 'throwing out the baby with the bathwater' and some people are never able to react appropriately or spontaneously to, say, a traumatic or sexual situation. Such people are somehow 'different' or even experienced as unreal.

States of confusion
Indecision and other ruminative states of puzzled vagueness may be a way of distancing ourselves from unpleasant reality. Conflict and ambivalence, which can be painful, may be avoided in this way.

Sublimation
This is a so-called 'higher' solution, whereby anxieties become channelled into positive acts or ways of life, e.g. creativity, gardening (say), restoring objects and turning sadism into an occupation such as surgery. *It is worth repeating that defence mechanisms are present in us all and it is when they break down that symptoms may ensue.*

Oedipus complex

Freud did not invent this, but 'adapted' and extrapolated the scenario from the Greek myth wherein the hero unknowingly slays the parent of the same sex and espouses that of the opposite sex. As in Sophocles' drama, the phenomenon is unconscious. Present-day analysts, whilst still alert to the concept, are equally vigilant to evidence of disturbances at an earlier, or pre-oedipal, time, i.e. when the baby's preoccupation is with the mother (a two-person relationship) rather than later, when the third person (father) has entered the drama.

Transference

This is an ubiquitous and everyday phenomenon between persons. Attitudes, feelings and ideas from the past towards significant people become trans-ferred to acquaintances and even friends in the present, often without justification. It is, however, the most important *tool* in psychoanalysis and psychoanalytical psychotherapy, as the patient may invest the therapist with what may well be totally inappropriate characteristics and attitudes, which can be changed or at least modified during the therapy and, by extrapolation, a more realistic appraisal of people in the patient's world may become established. In particular, strangers and acquaintances become less endowed with initial hostility and threat, so that more propitious feelings between the patient and his or her objects can become established.

Countertransference

This is the equivalent in the therapist. This will include the therapist's blind-spots of which cognisance and knowledge must be present. Its existence makes a personal therapy on the part of the doctor highly desirable, some would say essential. Countertransference feelings can also mirror attitudes, both conscious and unconscious, originating in the patient, but experienced and recognised in the therapist. With proper timing they may be conveyed to the patient as an aid to the two people's joint understanding.

The unconscious

This refers to both the part of the mind about which the subject is unaware and processes that are not within consciousness. Its existence is suggested by three phenomena:

1. Dreams.
2. Posthypnotic suggestion.
3. Slips of the tongue.

Unconscious processes are linked to what Freud called primary processes. These are primitive and unstructured methods of mental functioning: they reduce unpleasure or pain and promote *pleasure*. Images become fused and can readily replace and symbolise each other, as in dreams. *Secondary process* thinking, on the other hand, is logical, orderly and bound up with reality, reducing 'unpleasure' or pain, by adaptation.

Projective identification

This is a term from the Kleinian schools which is being found to have increasing usefulness (Jureidini, 1990). It is at once a defence mechanism whereby feelings are projected onto the object (therapist) who is at the same time identified with. The latter will also have the impression that a communication of the subject's feelings has become part of his or her own mental experience. For example, a doctor may repeatedly feel hopeless, irritable or even angry whenever a given patient is seen and it may be useful tactfully to 'share' these negative affects with the patient, saying something like, 'it is sometimes difficult to feel optimistic and encouraged and at the moment I have no such feelings. I suspect it is how *you* often feel . . .'. Far from being discouraging, the patient may well experience a lessening of his or her isolation and such an exchange may form the basis of more propitious future dialogues.

References

COLTART, N.E.C. (1988). The assessment of psychological-mindedness in the diagnostic interview. *British Journal of Psychiatry* **153**, 819–820.

HOUSTON, W.R. (1938). The doctor himself as a therapeutic agent. *Annals of Internal Medicine* **11**, 1416–1425.

JUREIDINI, F. (1990). Projective identification in general psychiatry. *British Journal of Psychiatry* **157**, 656–660.

Chapter 2
Psychodynamic Therapy

DAVID A. ALEXANDER

History and Development

The profession of psychotherapy is rewarding, both intellectually and emotionally. Its practice can also be taxing and difficult and, as is the case with other specialties dealing with people, its injudicious application can be harmful. Therefore, it demands an unusually high degree of personal integrity on the part of its practitioners. Unfortunately, psychotherapists must share a collective responsibility for failing in the past to pay sufficient attention to the harmful effects of their treatment methods and to the ethical issues related thereto. It is therefore encouraging to find that major attempts have now been made to address such matters (e.g. Mays and Franks, 1985; Lakin, 1988).

Over the last 50 years, schools of psychotherapy have multiplied in such a way that aspirants to the profession are faced with a bewildering array of approaches. In the absence of a comprehensive body of convincing empirical data to justify the claims of one school against those of another, it is difficult to decide which theories and techniques to adopt. In fact, despite what we might like to believe, many clinicians ally themselves to a particular form of therapy for motives that have little to do with logic or evaluative research. Powerful determinants of their choice include personal prejudice and serendipity (Nemiroff and Colarusso, 1985; Alexander and Eagles, 1990).

Nonetheless, whatever the factors underlying the choice of model, practitioners should always consider what they are doing to their patients and why. More specifically, they should be in a position to answer five basic questions. The answers to these questions will expose important assumptions underlying their particular choice of therapy. These questions are:

1. What factors influence human behaviour?
2. What are the basic aims of this therapy?

3. What are the characteristic features of the therapeutic relationship?
4. What are the techniques and skills associated with this therapy?
5. What problems or patients can best be helped by this therapy?

In this chapter, each of these questions will be addressed in relation to the psychodynamic model. Before doing so, however, some of the important historical features of this model should be looked at in order to provide a background against which these questions can be more appropriately considered.

Most forms of psychotherapy almost certainly owe something to Sigmund Freud (1856–1939) and to the treatment called 'psychoanalysis' which he developed and which has served as the prototype for later psychodynamic therapies. This does not mean that Freud 'invented' psychotherapy or that all his ideas were entirely novel. On the contrary, many of his concepts and ideas have very long pedigrees. For instance, the notion of a 'talking cure' (as psychoanalysis has been called), achieved through the verbal expression of pent-up feelings, is closely related to the Catholic 'confessional'. It can also be traced to the use of the theatre in ancient Greece as a public means of 'purging the passions'. However, whilst it is important to be aware of the ancestry of some of our current ideas and practices, the fact that we can identify their medical and cultural antecedents in no way devalues the signal contribution of Freud and the early analysts. Such has been the indelible and widespread influence of psychoanalytical ideas that they have fertilised developments, not only in medical psychology and psychiatry, but also in the social sciences and in the arts. Psychoanalysis has offered a form of treatment for certain mental disorders as well as a distinctive view of human beings, their behaviour and their development.

Inevitably, certain features of this widespread movement attracted a good deal of opposition and criticism. Analytical propositions were attacked on the grounds that they were formulated too closely to be amenable to verification or refutation by traditional scientific procedures. It is hardly surprising that this objection was raised, because the late nineteenth and early twentieth centuries had seen many notable advances in the physical sciences, and 'verifiability' and 'refutability' were acclaimed as the two most important criteria of the integrity and status of a proposition or theory.

Another related criticism was that the 'evidence' offered by clinicians to support their claims was nothing more than unsubstantiated hearsay and anecdotes: it was the product of private activities and experience occurring in the consulting room. Theorists and clinicians espousing other models, the 'behaviourists' in particular, have consistently argued that those who practise a psychodynamic form of therapy seem to have been unacceptably reluctant to evaluate the process and outcome of their therapeutic work and to adhere to the conventional canons of scientific enquiry.

Criticisms such as these should not be dismissed readily or be upheld slavishly. There are some major and specific difficulties in carrying out investigative and evaluative research in this area, and it is questionable whether the study of human behaviour can be carried out in the same way as someone might study, for example, the love life of an amoeba! However, it cannot be disputed that there is a dearth of studies into the process, concepts and therapeutic value of psychodynamic therapy. There is also a need to remove some of the mystery and veneration which surrounds this form of therapy. Illusory concepts, abstruse reasoning and a pseudoscientific jargon may be intriguing or even reassuring to some, but such things probably contribute nothing to the welfare of patients or to the development of our understanding of human behaviour and experience.

Whatever the 'scientific' status of psychoanalysis, however, its significance in the history of Western thought is not in doubt, and this fact has much to do with the personal contribution of Freud himself. It is therefore fitting to make some brief reference to his personal and intellectual life.

Despite his enormous contribution to clinical work, Freud was a reluctant therapist and physician. His reasons for embarking on a medical career were more pragmatic than idealistic – being a medical practitioner was more lucrative than being a physiologist – and his ambitions were more academic than humanitarian. His main aim was to produce a general theory of human behaviour and, in pursuit of this aim, he regarded himself first as a scientist and only secondly as a clinician. Being a compassionate man by nature, however, Freud did not sacrifice his patients' welfare in the furtherance of his own academic aspirations as a psychologist.

His intellectual integrity, not to say courage, cannot be questioned. Throughout his career a willingness to let (as he put it) 'facts speak for themselves' even though, in doing so, he had to modify and relinquish some of his most fundamental propositions, such as that about the role of sexual trauma in the development of certain mental disorders. His willingness and, indeed, his determination to adhere to 'the facts' also led him to maintain certain views despite the resultant public and professional criticism and even odium. For example, Freud originally believed that sexual fantasies and attachments begin in early childhood and that the child obtains sexual satisfaction from different parts of his or her body as he or she develops. Moreover, he argued that early childhood sexual experiences continue to exert an effect in later life. If we think of the moral straitjacket imposed during the Victorian era on the public discussion of sexual matters, it is hardly surprising that these views met with disbelief and disapproval. A lesser man might easily have succumbed to the strong opposition and have relinquished his ideas; Freud did not.

His courage in holding to or modifying his theory in the light of empirical and clinical evidence was matched by his physical courage. In the last years of his life he was handicapped by terminal cancer of the jaw, but he continued his academic and clinical work despite this distressing and painful illness.

Moreover, in order that he might retain all his mental powers, he refused analgesics for this condition.

It was, however, his shrewdness and sensitivity as an observer of human behaviour that led to major developments in his theory about human beings. Generally, it was not that he saw different things from other people, but rather that he saw the same things differently. The capacity to reformulate old ideas and synthesise common observations is, of course, the hallmark of the creative and outstanding scientist.

An opportunity to display this ability occurred when he attended the dramatic demonstrations by Dr Charcot in Paris. The purpose of these demonstrations was to show how patients, in response to hypnotic suggestion, could manifest symptoms which resembled neurological ones such as aphonia, paralysis and paraesthesia. Impressed as well as puzzled by these demonstrations, and yet firmly convinced about the enormous importance of psychological factors, Freud reflected on some of the patients who had been referred to him in Vienna for the treatment of similar conditions. He wondered if it might be possible that these symptoms had developed in response to the patients' own unconscious ideas – a form of 'autosuggestion'. He suspected that the patients would have been as unaware of the effect of their own ideas as Charcot's patients had been of his suggestions. Using hypnosis as a means of removing symptoms rather than as a means of inducing them, Freud found that hypnosis was an effective method of directly achieving symptom relief. Despite his initial success, however, he was troubled by the thought that, if he and the patient did not know what underlay the development of these symptoms then, whilst suggestion might produce some relief, it would only be temporary; either the influence of these unconscious ideas would begin to reassert itself and the symptoms would reappear, or other symptoms would emerge in their place. The second possibility has been described as 'symptom substitution'.

It was in the course of working with the Austrian physician Josef Breuer (with whom he wrote, in 1895, the seminal *Stüdien über Hysterie*) that Freud realised that there might be another way of using hypnosis, one which might offer a more durable cure or change (Breuer and Freud, 1964). Instead of using hypnosis as a means of achieving direct symptom relief, when the underlying cause remained unknown, Freud began to use it as a means of revealing and exploring what had given rise to the symptom in the first place. The possibility of using hypnosis in this way had been suggested to him by the fact that one of Breuer's patients (immortalised in the literature as 'Anna O') had been able, under hypnosis, to recall feelings and events previously inaccessible to her and, in doing so, she had been relieved of her symptoms. In brief, therefore, the aim was to treat the underlying cause and not just the symptoms, the latter being regarded as a breakthrough, in a disguised form, of 'blocked-off' or inhibited feelings.

At that time, Freud was proposing a radical approach because the prevailing view was a reductionist one: symptoms were held to be due to a disturbance in some physical or biochemical system. Freud, however, was claiming that many symptoms – both physical and mental – had a psychological cause and, moreover, that these symptoms had some personal and symbolic meaning for the patient. The patient is frequently unaware of this meaning or significance, and unaware of the link between the emotions and the symptoms. At this stage, it is interesting to consider how many common expressions and metaphors there are in our language which reflect the association between emotions and parts of the body. These include, 'he's a pain in the neck', 'she gets on my nerves', 'you're breaking my heart', 'he's a real headache to me' and 'that was a real body blow'.

It was this belief in the association between the underlying emotions and the overt symptoms that confirmed Freud's opinion that many mental disorders and, in particular, the neuroses could not be understood adequately or treated successfully using conventional medical concepts and procedures.

For a number of reasons, Freud gave up his use of hypnosis and developed a procedure known as 'free association', whereby the patients were encouraged to talk without fear of censure about their past experiences and their most private thoughts, wishes, fears and so forth. In their doing so, Freud believed that the patients and he would be able to unravel the connection between underlying but previously unrecognised factors and presenting symptoms. To hold this view, of course, assumes a 'psychological determinism' in that such a view implies that all aspects of behaviour and experience can be seen as outcomes of earlier mental or physical events. According to this view, symptoms do not appear by chance or caprice.

Although this procedure of free association was obviously a much more time-consuming one than hypnosis, Freud believed that the results obtained would be lasting. By helping the patient become aware of events, ideas and feelings, which previously had been unconscious, the effect of these phenomena in terms of symptom development would cease. Moreover, by resolving the underlying problem, symptom-substitution would not occur. For theorists, such as Kris (1987), free association is still regarded as having the central role in psychoanalytical treatment.

As might be expected, psychoanalysis in particular and psychodynamic theory in general have undergone many revisions and modifications since the days of Freud and his contemporaries. Some authorities, e.g. Sullivan (1953), played down the view of human beings as victims of turbulent internal and biological drives and, instead, focused on the nature of the individual's social relationships. Similarly, Erikson (1950) tried to recast psychoanalytical theory in terms of psychosocial concepts. He is particularly well known for his elaboration of the eight psychosocial stages of personality development and their associated psychosocial crises and conflict.

Despite these and other more recent developments, which will be covered in Chapter 3, strong traces of the more traditional Freudian notions reappear, sometimes under a different guise. To some extent this is the case with aspects of Berne's theory of transactional analysis (Berne, 1966). One of the key concepts generated by this theory is that of 'ego-states', of which Berne identified three: the 'child', the 'adult' and the 'parent'. These ego-states are discussed more fully in Chapter 3.

Before we leave this topic, one particular point which justifies repetition, is the importance of conflict. Obviously, theories about the nature of human beings abound. Some emphasise the physical and biological aspects, whilst others focus on the interpersonal and social influences, but the theme which tends to link all these theories is that of the potential for and importance of conflict. Indeed, the contribution of conflict to human diseases and dis-ease is a characteristic feature of psychodynamic theory. Some of these other developments will emerge as the five basic questions, which were raised earlier, are addressed.

What Factors influence Human Behaviour?

According to the psychodynamic view of mankind, our behaviour and experience are the result of a number of competing urges, wishes and other influences – some conscious, but others unconscious and therefore beyond our awareness. It is to these unconscious influences that much of psycho-dynamic therapy is directed. Indeed, one of the most influential concepts in the attempt to understand human behaviour and experience is that of unconscious motivation. Although there has been much debate about whether or not the unconscious is a legitimate concept and worthy of study, much psychological research (including that into 'selective attention' and 'subliminal perception') – quite independent of psychodynamic theory – has confirmed the need to acknowledge the influence of unconscious processes. In his earliest writings, Freud regarded the unconscious as a sovereign concept, a concept which included memories, impulses and ideas generally not available to conscious scrutiny, and he distinguished the unconscious from the 'preconscious' and the 'conscious'. The former he viewed as the repository of impulses, sense impressions and memories of which we are not immediately aware, but could easily be so if required or if the focus of our attention were suitably redirected. (For example, we are not normally aware of our clothes touching our bodies until something directs our attention to these sensations.) The conscious sphere of mental life, a more self-explanatory concept, corresponds to everything of which we are aware at any given time. It also includes therefore those aspects of ourselves to which we are prepared to admit (if only to ourselves), in contrast to those features, for instance of our personality or past, which we find less acceptable and which we relegate to the unconscious realm. (Although it is very convenient to talk in terms of the 'unconscious' and 'conscious' as though they had some spatial existence, this may be misleading. It is probably more accurate to think of all mental activity as occurring along a continuum of consciousness, ranging from complete unawareness to focal attentiveness.)

The distinction between conscious and unconscious mental activities is also associated with a differentiation between cognitive processes. The conscious level of functioning involves 'secondary processes', which are logical, rational and geared to meet the demands of the real world. In contrast, unconscious activities are associated with 'primary processes', which are not usually adapted to meet the demands of reality, but function to achieve the satisfaction of very basic and urgent needs or drives. We can catch glimpses of these more primitive aspects of ourselves and the processes associated with them when we are dreaming, are emotionally aroused or are under the influence of alcohol or other drugs. *In vino veritas* is therefore a particularly apt aphorism according to psychodynamic theory. Slips of the tongue and slips of the pen, collectively referred to as 'parapraxes' ('Freudian slips'), may also provide interesting and important clues to the presence of unconscious views, feelings and wishes, many of which we would not comfortably acknowledge in full consciousness. Anyone who is particularly interested in the topic of unconsciously motivated errors should, as well as reflecting on his or her own 'mistakes', read Freud's *The Psychopathology of Everyday Life* (1960).

In the 1920s, Freud revised his ideas about mental activity and its influence on human experience and behaviour. He offered a new model, a good deal of which still permeates much of our thinking and language, both lay and professional. This model is a more complex one, involving a tripartite division of the psyche into three elements: the id, the ego and the super-ego. Despite its greater complexity, it has the advantage of trying to embrace biological, experimental, interpersonal and social aspects of human life.

The first of these elements, the id, on the one hand represents all the inherited, biological and constitutional features of the individual, including instincts and basic drives, such as those pertaining to eating, aggression, sex and elimination. These forces, Freud believed, operate according to the hedonistic pleasure principle in that they avoid being frustrated and seek immediate gratification, regardless of the consequences. On the other hand, the super-ego is very much concerned with the consequences of our actions, since it is built up from internalised representations of the standards and ideals upheld by others who are particularly important to us. Living as we do in relationships with others, we have to conform to many social and cultural standards, and it is through the super-ego that many of these standards are transmitted and perpetuated. As a result of our dislike of rejection, censure or punishment, we tend to conform to many of the expectations of others, especially those whom we hold in high regard or who have authority over us. For most of us, the first 'culture' to which we are exposed is that of our own family and, consequently, much of our super-ego development reflects the impact of parental values and ideals.

The third element, the ego, roughly corresponds to the conscious level of functioning. It develops progressively from birth – according to some authorities, it does so from an even earlier stage – and its first task is to distinguish between the inner world of subjective experience and external reality; or, to put it another way, it tries to distinguish between 'I' and 'not I'. The ego is reality oriented, and therefore it has to find acceptable and appropriate ways of satisfying the demands of the id, although this means that, at least temporarily, the gratification of the id must be delayed. For example, if we are ravenously hungry, the id drives us to find some immediate way of obtaining food, perhaps by theft or deception, but to do so would be socially unacceptable. Realistically, we can also see that it is likely to lead to further difficulties for us: for instance, we might be caught or we might harm others in the process. Thus, the ego tries to ensure that the satisfaction of such a need is sufficiently delayed to allow us to find some reasonable and socially acceptable means of finding food and satisfying the urge to eat. On other occasions, the ego has to appease the demands of the super-ego. Although the super-ego can be helpful by keeping us out of trouble (rather like the lay person's concept of conscience), it can also act as a source of primitive, irrational and punitive morality and idealism. Consequently, instead of guiding us helpfully, the super-ego may unnecessarily restrict and inhibit our behaviour, feelings and personal development. This may be seen in those individuals who are totally dominated by their need to do 'the right thing' and to avoid upsetting others.

In other words, the ego may have to act as an arbiter in the face of the competing demands of the id and the super-ego; not an easy task, because the demands of one element may be as clamorous, irrational and pressing as those of the other. Sometimes, the effectiveness of the ego can be substantially reduced or modified by the effects of alcohol, sensory deprivation, insomnia or powerful emotions. Consequently, mental activity, experiences and behaviour occurring during these altered states of awareness appear to be less censored, less rational and more under the influence of the pleasure principle. Some dreams may also show the signs of reduced ego involvement, and it is not surprising that Freud described dreams as 'the royal road to the unconscious'.

Freud had great difficulty in deciding what the basic human drives and instincts were – a difficulty, we should note, that he shared with most other theorists. He settled for the notion that there were two mainsprings driving human behaviour: these were the 'life instincts' and the 'death instincts' (conventionally referred to as 'eros' and 'thanatos' respectively). The latter group he regarded as basically destructive in that they seek to reduce us to inorganic matter. The life instincts, however, try to maintain life: in this capacity, one of these instincts – the sexual instinct – plays a particularly significant role. At first, Freud believed that the sexual instinct was served exclusively by a form of energy called the 'libido', but later he concluded that all life instincts drew from this source.

Although Freud was particularly impressed by the frequency with which conflict occurred over sexual matters, what is more important to note is not the nature of the instincts themselves, but rather their potential for creating competing influences on human behaviour and thereby providing a source of conflict. In Freud's view, we are constantly being pulled and pushed in different directions by equally powerful but mutually antagonistic forces. Thus, behind human experience and behaviour, there lies a constantly shifting dynamic of forces between which we are always trying to achieve some equilibrium. As applied to psychology, the term 'dynamic', borrowed from nineteenth-century physics and physiology, reflects this particular view. Freud was very impressed with the notion of forces competing with one another and he was aware that, in physics, the resolution of the opposition between two competing forces was sometimes achieved by the emergence of a third force which moves off in a completely different direction from the other two. In terms of human behaviour and experience, the equivalent of the emergence of the third force would be the development of a symptom. According to this theory, symptom formation is not therefore a random or inexplicable event, but a means of relieving what would other-wise be intolerable and interminable conflict, i.e. a compromise, a 'solution' that is the *least unacceptable* to all the forces concerned: id, ego and reality.

The importance of the concept of conflict is obvious if we think how often depression, anxiety and physical symptoms, such as headaches, 'low back pain' and stomach upsets, develop when we are racked with doubts involving opposites: 'Will I, won't I?', 'Did I, didn't I?' and 'Can I, can't I?'. There are, of course, many other conflicts whose source may not be obvious to us; the conflict remains at an unconscious level and we only become aware of the symptoms to which it has given rise.

Some conflicts may be quite transient, whereas others may trouble us throughout our lives, and some may be more characteristic of certain stages of our development. The resolution of some conflicts may be only partial and their impact may be experienced from time to time, particularly when we are under stress. A good example of this, according to psychoanalytical theory, is that of the oedipal conflict. It is believed that children (at least those in Western society) between the ages of 3 and 4 years develop a strong attachment to the parent of the opposite sex. This gives rise to feelings of rivalry towards the parent of the same sex, who in turn becomes a source of threat and retaliation. It is argued that these feelings of attraction, and the conflict associated with them, are never thoroughly resolved and we are likely to experience echoes of this early conflict throughout our lives as we forge new relationships. This may account for the fact that some of our relationships in adult life repeat the dynamics evident in our own family.

The significance of conflict also sired much of the thinking of Moreno (1953) whose name is usually associated with 'psychodrama'. He argued that, throughout life, we are required to enact different roles, depending on the different social contexts in which we find ourselves. Sometimes, we have to play the role of the passive, tolerant husband, sometimes the forceful, authoritative teacher and at other times the kindly, caring clinician. Not surprisingly, these roles can conflict with each other.

What are the Basic Aims of this Therapy?
(see also p. 45)

One of the earliest forms of therapy for mental illness was catharsis, and this was used long before a humane approach towards the mentally ill was adopted. Catharsis (or, as it is sometimes called, 'abreaction') prevailed as a means of 'treatment' even when mental disorder was attributed to demoniacal possession. A cathartic experience can be defined as one in which there is an uninhibited and often dramatic expression of pent-up feelings, achieved by the relating and/or 'reliving' of significant past experiences, or sometimes by the acting out of anticipated events or experiences. The alleged value of this is captured in lay expressions – 'letting off steam', 'getting it off your chest' and 'getting it out of your system'.

In the absence of this emotional release, it was believed that the uncomfortable feelings would continue to build up emotional pressure until finally they would 'leak out' or, worse still, 'erupt' in some maladaptive way, such as through the development of mental and/or physical ill health. This view certainly has an intuitive appeal and no doubt catharsis does effect some relief, but the theory upon which the use of catharsis or abreaction is based may owe more to vulcanology than it does to psychology. It is not that giving vent to feelings has no value: the doubt is that it may offer only short-term, symptomatic relief rather than long-term improvement and durable change. One argument raised is that, in the absence of patients understanding thoroughly why they behave and feel the way they do, and feeling they have gained control over the original experience, there will only be a short-term remission of symptoms followed by a re-emergence of them or the development of new ones. This harks back to the notion of 'symptom-oriented' vs 'problem-oriented' treatment which arose in the consideration of the historical development of psychodynamic therapy.

Insight or self-awareness is not usually a quality with which most of us are over-endowed. People tend to build up their own private view of themselves and of their world, and often this view turns out to be highly deceptive and inconsistent with the view held by others. Sometimes the discrepancy may be quite innocuous or humorous; but unfortunately it can also be the basis of a good deal of unhappiness and, worse still, illness. For example, if for reasons which lie deep in the past, a patient were to see the world as a place full of threat, hostility and rejection, he might try to defend himself by withdrawing from human relationships, trusting nobody and rejecting others before they can reject him. This is hardly a formula for interpersonal success, and he would run the considerable risk of ending up feeling depressed, unloved, lonely and frustrated.

In this patient's case, the aim of therapy would be to help him to understand the role of his previous, unhappy personal relationships in the development of this jaundiced view of life and of his symptoms. He would have to learn to accept, therefore, some responsibility for his feelings, for his view of the world and for his symptoms. This should be a learning process and not a confession. To a psychiatrist with a psychodynamic orientation, other treatment options such as medication, electroconvulsive therapy and many forms of behaviour therapy could be seen as less appropriate, on the grounds that they would be aiming at symptom relief, leaving the 'real' problem untouched.

Unfortunately, even the provision of insight and the opportunity for catharsis do not guarantee behavioural change. There are various factors that make it difficult to behave in different ways and to 'give up' symptoms – despite new insights. One reason is that changing our ways and presenting ourselves differently to the world, like any form of change, carries with it a risk that things might turn out to be even worse. It is sometimes a matter of the devil you know being rather safer than the one you do not know. For example, some patients fear that if they reveal their feelings or certain facets of their personalities which they had previously hidden from themselves as well as from others, then there is a risk that other people will find them unacceptable and even less desirable.

Ego Defence Mechanisms

Another important aim of therapy should therefore be to help the patient adapt to changes in functioning and attitudes which therapy has brought about. The value of this aim is particularly evident when the patient is required to give up or modify certain coping strategies called *ego defence mechanisms*. These are particularly important concepts in psychodynamic theory, and it will be valuable to consider them in some detail. To emphasise their dynamic and adaptive nature, it would probably be more appropriate to use the word 'processes' rather than the word 'mechanisms'. However, the latter – probably again reflecting the influence of the physical sciences – has gained such a secure foothold in the language of psychodynamics that it will continue to be used here.

The purpose of these defences is to protect us (or our egos) from being disturbed or, worse, being overwhelmed by our emotions – anxiety being the most obvious and common example. Anxiety may be created by external factors, such as separation, loss, illness and trauma, but it may also be created by internal ones, such as ideas, wishes, emotions and memories. The protection offered by these mechanisms comes from the fact that they enable us to distort, reject, transform or inhibit our awareness of feelings, ideas, sense impressions and other things which might threaten our self-esteem and composure. Generally, these defences operate at an unconscious level such that we are unaware of what it is that evokes the defence. They should not therefore be regarded as conscious attempts to lie or deceive.

Many defence mechanisms have been described in the clinical and theoretical literature, and a particularly illuminating account of some of them is provided by Anna Freud (1936) in her valuable text *The Ego and the Mechanisms of Defence*. It is also worth noting that these concepts have attracted considerable support from experimental psychologists, and various methods have been devised to measure them (Vaillant, 1986).

For present purposes five commonly observed defences will be described. These will demonstrate how such defences enable us to cope with reality.

Repression

This is the process whereby disturbing ideas, memories or feelings which threaten to become conscious are retained at, or relegated to, an unconscious level. A good example of repression was provided by a patient of mine who, as a child, suffered very serious burns to the throat and neck because of carelessness on the part of her mother. Ten years have passed and the patient is still quite unable to recall anything about the incident or its sequelae, requiring intravenous feeding and extensive skin grafting. The family have never discussed with the patient what actually happened; instead, it is as though the accident had never happened. Interestingly, her presenting symptom was an inability to swallow food in public places because, as she said 'It sticks in my throat'.

To refer to her problem of recall as 'mere forgetfulness' would be to ignore the fact that to recollect the incident and describe it would necessitate her being reminded of the full horror, pain, distress and anger associated with the episode. It is not difficult, therefore, to understand why this girl had 'blocked off' this dreadful incident in her life.

Projection

Another means of dealing with uncomfortable emotions or attitudes is to resist acknowledging them within oneself and to attribute them to others. This is called projection. For example, if a person found it difficult to accept his or her own capacity to be hostile and rejecting, one way to resolve this would be to 'project' (unconsciously) this characteristic on to others, allowing the person thereby to accuse these individuals of being angry and rejecting towards him or her. An extreme form of this process can be seen in patients who suffer from a disorder called paranoia. Paranoid patients are characteristically hypersensitive to what they consider to be humiliation or rebuffs. By means of projection, they tend to distort their perception of what would have been entirely innocuous or friendly actions and comments by others, and view them as challenging and hostile. Their belief that the world is an aggressive and threatening place then appears to provide paranoid patients with justification for taking retaliatory action. Because patients see themselves as merely reacting to the aggressiveness of others, their own anger and even violence will then seem entirely justifiable to them and no longer threatening to their own self-image.

Displacement

Scapegoating is a well-known method of ridding oneself of frustration and anger. In psychodynamic terms, this is referred to as displacement. For instance, if a doctor were extremely angry with one of his patients, but felt unable to express this feeling directly to the patient, one way to deal with this uncomfortable, pent-up emotion would be to redirect it towards his secretary. The doctor might complain, for instance, about some minor error or indiscretion which under other circumstances would have evoked no response from him. This redirection of the anger would make him feel better for two related reasons. First, he would have managed to rid himself of his anger and, secondly, he would have been able to do so in a way which did not threaten his own view of himself; a view which does not include being angry with patients.

Denial

Denial is another form of defence against anxiety and it refers to the inability of the individual to acknowledge some reality. Commonly, it is displayed by relatives who have just been informed of the sudden and unexpected death of a loved one: 'Oh, she can't be dead!' is a characteristic response. It may also be seen in people who have a serious or life-threatening illness and yet refuse to recognise the significance of their symptoms, and avoid seeking the appropriate help, despite apparently incontrovertible and substantial evidence to support the diagnosis. It might also be considered that members of the family of the badly burned patient referred to earlier were displaying denial by behaving as though the accident had never occurred.

Somatisation

In a textbook such as this, somatisation must be included among the mechanisms of defence. Even today it is more acceptable to our *amour propre* to present to a doctor with, say, asthma, migraine, indigestion or hypertension than with recurrent anxiety states, depressions or, worse, psychotic breakdowns. It is not surprising, therefore, to find that many emotional problems are translated into physical symptoms. It is important for doctors, as a consequence, to try to understand what might lie behind certain physical ailments, particularly when they are resistant to those physical treatments that would normally be effective.

Before we move on from the topic of ego defence mechanisms, three points should be underlined and noted. The first is that we all use such defences – it is not just patients who do so – because they can be adaptive by providing a means of coping, if only temporarily, with events or feelings that would otherwise be too disturbing and disruptive. It is only when the defences themselves prove too 'costly' for the individual (in mental or physical terms), or to his or her environment in terms of antisocial behaviour, i.e. when the defences break down, that doctors or the judiciary may be involved. Medical students are often faced with anxiety-provoking situations which threaten their composure (Alexander and Haldane, 1979, 1980). For example, their first experience at the dissecting table can be very distressing and, as a consequence, a variety of defences is marshalled to protect them from this anxiety. As a temporary device, for example, denial of feelings may be a convenient protective shield through which reality can percolate at a rate at which the individual can adjust and adapt (see Chapter 4). It is only when such defences are used excessively and become more a way of life that, far from being adaptive and constructive, they can have a constricting and crippling effect on the development of the personality. This is the case with certain neurotic illnesses and personality disorders. Similarly, a problem can arise when the doctor's own emotional defences against anxiety block her perception and understanding of her patient's emotional problems. This may occur, for example, when the doctor's response to anxiety and discomfiture is to distance herself from her patient by being 'cool' and 'objective'. Such a reaction may give the patient the message that emotional expressions are unacceptable. This 'distancing' is too frequently seen in the case of terminally ill patients, because staff find it difficult to deal with such patients' emotional reactions (Alexander and Ritchie, 1990).

The second point is that, in therapy, insensitive assaults on these defences are not only likely to be unproductive therapeutically, but may even be damaging to the patient. Unfortunately, for some doctors the glimpse of a defence mechanism displayed by patients seems to arouse a missionary zeal, a *furor therapeuticus*, which inspires them to demolish the defence and try to 'deal with' the underlying anxiety. It is a bit like kicking a crutch away from a man with a broken leg and then looking puzzled, if not aggrieved, because he falls down in pain rather than offering his profuse thanks. A clinical case demonstrates this most clearly. A former patient of mine in the throes of a serious puerperal illness tried to end her own life by setting fire to herself with paint stripper. She survived, but with very obvious and major disfigurement to the head, chest and face. Initially, she made no effort to disguise her disfigurement by the use of a hair piece, cosmetics or carefully chosen clothing. She was showing denial. Some of the nursing staff and the other patients in the ward sought to 'confront' her (sometimes rather forcefully) to accept the extent of her disfigurement and to take steps to disguise it. This rather insensitive approach simply provoked further denial, because this unfortunate woman needed time to adapt gradually to what she had done to herself. (An interesting question is, of course, whose anxieties was all this confrontation aimed at – the puerperal patient's or those of the staff and the other patients?) The defences must be respected. A more therapeutic aim would be to help the patient to use her defence in a flexible and constructive way. Moreover, if the patient can be helped to identify gradually what it is that she needs to be defended from, then other more adaptive and constructive means of dealing with the threat might be found.

The third and final point is that the protection offered by such defences is rarely foolproof. Powerful conflicts and feelings have a tendency to 'leak out' into consciousness, and may present themselves at the most inappropriate time and in the most inappropriate way. One doctor became acutely aware of this at the end of a supervision session, in which she had been confronted by me about her tendency to 'forget' what I had repeatedly told her. She stated, 'It's not that I try to remember, eh, I mean, to forget what you tell me'.

What are the Characteristic Features of the Therapeutic Relationship?

The 'contract'

Despite the variety of theories embraced by the psychodynamic model, there does seem to be a consensus about the crucial role of the relationship between the doctor and the patient. First and foremost, it is a *professional* relationship, however caring and dedicated the clinician. Because of this, there are limits to what may take place between the doctor and the patient: it is a case of disciplined intimacy. To some extent the limits are determined by the aims of therapy, because the purpose of the relationship is to foster and facilitate activities and conditions that are therapeutic or potentially therapeutic.

As in other professional relationships, there should be a mutually agreed 'contract' between the two parties. In other words, the doctor *and* the patient should be aware of what it is they are seeking to do and how they are going to achieve this. Not only does the establishment of a 'contract' help to ensure that their work together is purposeful, but the process of defining the goals can be helpful to the patient. If we cannot explain to our patient what we are going to do and how it might help, we should not start treatment. Patients often come feeling so overwhelmed by their symptoms and problems that helping them to define and identify what has to be done, and why, is itself an important and reassuring step in the treatment. The restoration of hope and clarity is no mean achievement.

Transference and countertransference

One of Freud's earliest observations was that, in the course of therapy, patients developed strong emotions towards him. Freud assumed these reactions to be unrealistic and related to the patients' experiences in earlier relationships, particularly those with their parents. 'Transference' was the technical term he introduced to describe this tendency of patients to direct to him feelings and attitudes which would have been more appropriately directed to other significant persons in their lives. At first, transference was regarded as a barrier to treatment, but Freud soon realised that understanding the transference reaction was a valuable way of gaining insight into how patients distorted their view of themselves and of others. Thereafter, many therapists saw the understanding and analysis of the transference as the major focus of psychoanalytical therapy.

Transference feelings may be positive or negative, and often there is a mixture of both. Positive transference can be seen in the way the patient describes his or her doctor, for example, in unrealistically glowing terms, and also in the way he or she tries to translate the professional relationship into a social and personal one. 'Chance' meetings carefully contrived by the patient, or suggestions to extend the number of appointments, may indicate the patient's positive transference. Negative transference may be shown by expressions of hostility and rejection, by failure to keep appointments, by persistent unpunctuality or requests for a second opinion.

The therapeutic relationship can therefore be seen as a microcosm of the patient's world of interpersonal relationships – past, present and future. It provides an opportunity for the close and systematic analysis of how the patient behaves in relationships, his expectations, his needs and his defences. In addition, the therapeutic relationship serves as a testing-ground, or an interpersonal 'laboratory', in which the patient can explore and experiment with other ways of coping in relationships. For example, the patient may learn to express better her anger and other feelings which she has feared ventilating in the past. It is for this reason that this form of therapy has been described as an exercise in 'reparenting'. There is, however, nothing intrinsically therapeutic in the occurrence of transference: the crucial factor is the way in which transference develops to a degree in all relationships, but it is easy to see why it is more likely to occur where there is ambiguity and an opportunity for misinterpretation in a relationship. Although the rather passive and enigmatic figure of the psychotherapist is a rich vein of humour for cartoonists and satirists, this masterly inactivity is not a mere façade but a purposeful tactic. By deliberately limiting the extent to which his own feelings and values intrude in the therapeutic relationship, and by reflecting back to the patient those feelings and values she has 'transferred' to the therapeutic relationship, the doctor has an excellent means of helping the patient to understand how she perceives (or misperceives) herself and her relationship with others. Obviously, it would be unrealistic to imagine that any doctor could present himself as a completely 'blank screen'. Each therapeutic relationship is unique, and each will evoke some of the doctor's own characteristics and qualities, but the aim is to minimise the extent to which these interfere with the emergence of transference.

A corollary to this description of the stance to be adopted by the doctor is that he or she must resist the temptation to satisfy the patient's neurotic needs, especially those for love and affection. This can be difficult. It is not comfortable being seen by patients as unloving, uncaring and rejecting, when you are dedicated to helping them. Sometimes, the temptation is very strong for the doctor to 'correct' the patient's misinterpretation of what he or she is trying to do and of what sort of person the doctor is. I have found myself wanting to say to some of my terminal patients, 'There is no point in getting angry with me, I'm just doing my best'. This has to be resisted, however, because the anger the patients show towards me is not intended personally; it is the anger of a patient who perhaps feels cheated out of a normal life or who feels angry with doctors who failed to diagnose the malignancy earlier. It is also possible to 'prove' to the patient that we care by creating a highly dependent relationship in which the patient feels secure and shielded from all responsibilities. Although it perhaps offers temporary respite for the patient, this solves nothing in the long run, because the doctor has colluded in recreating in therapy the type of relationship in which the patient usually becomes trapped and which usually turns out to be self-defeating and unsatisfying. The doctor has behaved a bit like the parent who never allows the child to grow up and tries to satisfy every infantile need 'in order to keep him happy'.

As is the case with all therapeutic tools, the therapeutic relationship can be put to bad as well as good use. For instance, the relationship does provide the clinician with an opportunity for being punitive and hostile to his or her patient under the apparently respectable guise of a therapeutic tactic. Alternatively, the neurotic dependence and flattery of the patient may not be recognised for what they are, and the doctor may unhelpfully and unthinkingly exploit them. A doctor who constantly needs to be flattered and rewarded by his or her patients is likely to become the victim of this need to be gratified. It is more helpful if the doctor tries to understand what lies behind the patient's incessant need to please him or her. There are many possible motives – these include seducing the doctor into trying to solve the patient's problems, frustrating therapy and distracting the doctor from the principal task.

The issue of the doctor's feelings towards the patient inroduces another important concept – countertransference. In the same way that patients bring their past interpersonal experiences into the therapeutic relationship, doctors may also tend to react to their patients in terms of their own experiences in previous relationships: this tendency is known as 'countertransference'. As with transference, countertransference may be positive or negative. Psychotherapists may display negative countertransference by subtle (or sometimes not so subtle!) denigration of their patients, by making impossible or conflicting demands on them, or by 'forgetting' what patients had said the previous week. Positive countertransference may be revealed in various ways, including the offer of additional sessions or extension of sessions well beyond the allocated time. There was the case of one particular colleague of mine who even said 'Thank you' to his particularly attractive patient at the end of the therapy sessions! Once he became aware of his own unconscious feelings, however, he was able to use countertransference as a barometer of what was going on in therapy. In this way, countertransference can serve as a useful function: it is not something we need to fear and disclaim. It may be helpful on occasions to share your own feelings with the patient. A doctor saying, 'I'm feeling a bit confused by this and I'm not sure where we should go from here – maybe that's the way you're feeling too' is not an unprofessional admission of incompetence. On the contrary, it conveys an empathic understanding of the patient's feelings and indicates the honesty of the doctor as well as his or her willingness to continue to face the patient's problems.

The potential influence of countertransference therefore demands a good deal of basic self-awareness and a willingness to scrutinise our own behaviour and feelings in our relationships with patients. It is in recognition of this need that some authorities advocate that the doctor who wishes to practise dynamic psychotherapy should undergo a training analysis, or at least some form of personal therapeutic experience (although it has been pointed out by Macaskill (1983) that there does not seem to be persuasive evidence to indicate that personal therapy has much impact on clinical skills). Certainly, the significance of countertransference makes the need for supervision of therapy very obvious. Didactic teaching and reading can only give us a superficial awareness of the issues involved, but it is worth reading Wolstein's (1988) edited series of articles on countertransference, its evolution and relevance.

Whilst most clinicians would acknowledge the ubiquity and general importance of transference and countertransference, these terms have unfortunately been the subject of many definitions which have resulted in confusion rather than clarity. For example, one extreme view espoused by the Kleinian school of therapy is that *all* the interactions between doctor and patient are a product of transference and countertransference. Apart from the fact that this is not a testable proposition, attribution of all this to these concepts makes them appear to explain so much and yet they in fact explain nothing. According to the proposition, all behaviour and experiences would merely be a replay of earlier patterns of behaviour and experience. It is probably more helpful, therefore, to restrict the use of 'transference' to refer to those *inappropriate* feelings and attitudes that the patient develops towards the doctor *in the course of therapy*, because he distorts his image of the doctor in the light of his earlier experiences in important relationships. (The patient is firmly convinced, of course, that his own reactions are entirely appropriate to the circumstance.) Countertransference can then be viewed as the complement to the patient's transference. If, as their relationship developed, a patient were to begin to respond to the doctor in a child-like and dependent way, as though the doctor were a parent, then this would be interpreted as transference. If, in response to this form of behaviour from the patient, the doctor began treating him as though he were a dependent child, then this would be a case of countertransference. The use of these more restricted definitions allows us to acknowledge the occurrence of non-transference and non-countertransference reactions between the therapist and the patient. We must not forget that there are two real people engaged in a real relationship.

The therapeutic alliance

More recently, increased attention has been given to another element in the therapeutic relationship and that is what is called the 'therapeutic alliance'. Freud and the early analysts were aware of the importance of this feature, but they regarded it as another aspect of transference. Perhaps it is easier to consider that there are two 'parts' of the patient. The first 'part' is sick, unhappy and yet resistant to change, whereas the other 'part' is hopeful, cooperative and willing to change. It is with the second 'part' of the patient that the doctor has to ally him- or herself. In this way, the patient becomes an active agent in his or her own treatment, rather than behaving as a passive recipient of the clinician's skills and care. This is not the same, however, as describing the patient as being 'well motivated' for therapy: many patients are keen to 'get better' but their expectations may be quite unrealistic and based on the assumption that the improvement in their health or circumstances is solely the responsibility of the doctor. (Of course, patients should not be blamed for this expectation, because it is what they have been taught to expect from a traditional doctor–patient relationship). As part of the therapeutic alliance, the patient must achieve a realistic view of what the doctor can and should offer, and become aware of the extent to which a successful outcome will depend on his own efforts to help himself. The patient must also be willing to tolerate periods of frustration, disillusionment and emotional discomfort. Unfortunately, this is too much for some patients and they take what is described as a 'flight into health', reporting after only a few interviews that they are 'cured' and leaving, with expressions of profuse gratitude to their very talented and kindly doctor! Achieving a therapeutic alliance is probably easier if the doctor and the patient like each other, but this is not essential. Mutual trust and respect are probably more important: they have to be earned.

This section would not be complete if the issue of the termination of therapy were not mentioned. The end of the therapeutic relationship is an event of signal importance, particularly if the relationship has been of some months' duration, as is frequently the case. Indeed, it is in recognition of its importance that it is generally argued that termination should be built into the plans for therapy. Under ideal circumstances, we would like the end of therapy to be the natural outcome of the achievements of the therapeutic goals. Unfortunately, this is frequently not the reason for the end of therapy. Many factors conspire to produce a premature termination: these include the waning motivation of the patient, the departure from the region of the patient or the doctor, and significant changes in the patient's circumstances. However, whilst accepting that many terminations are not 'ideal', the clinician should always consider, when formulating with the patient the goals of therapy, what criteria would be used to decide when therapy should be terminated.

What are the Techniques and Skills associated with this Therapy?

One of Freud's patients aptly described psychoanalysis as the 'talking cure' and, from the time Freud stopped using hypnosis, the bedrock of the psychodynamic therapies has been the verbal interchange between the patient and the doctor. Non-verbal behaviour is certainly important as a dimension of communication, but even this usually has to be dealt with verbally at some stage. Most of the talking is done by the patient, particularly if the psychotherapist is encouraging the use of free association. Despite the trusting and facilitating atmosphere and relationship, talking in this un-inhibited way can be arduous and stressful for the patient, and he or she will often show signs of reluctance to continue. A similar reluctance may be shown by the patient to grasp what the doctor has suggested or to stick to the therapeutic contract. 'Resistance' is the technical term used to describe such efforts of the patient to maintain the status quo and to avoid proceeding with therapy. It is not at all helpful merely to criticise or disparage the patient because he or she shows signs of resistance. Also these signs of resistance should not be taken as confirmation that the patient does not want to help. Instead, the doctor should try to understand, and help the patient to understand, the source of the anxiety that lies behind the resistance. Most of us find it difficult to reveal very personal material, however trustworthy and receptive the audience but, from the point of view of therapy, it is often those things which the patient fears to disclose that provide the essential material for therapy.

We are not, however, powerless in the face of patients' resistance. We can make use of four techniques: confrontation, clarification, interpretation and 'working through'. These are the basic tools of psychodynamic therapy to be used to facilitate communication, to enhance understanding, to encourage the expression of feelings and to foster durable change.

'Confrontation', as the name suggests, means directing the patient's attention to something that he has done, said or experienced, but of which his awareness of having done it, or at least his awareness of its significance, is minimal. This technique should not be seen as a justification for bullying or being rude to patients. 'Have you ever noticed that each time just before your wife goes away on her own your asthma tends to play up?' would be an example of appropriate confrontation.

Another technique for increasing the patient's awareness is that of 'clarification', i.e. teasing out the relevant from the irrelevant features of the material presented by the patient. This may be done by rephrasing or reflecting back to the patient what she has said, or by skilfully questioning around a particular theme or issue.

'Interpretation' is a rather more complicated technique and one that has become a source of conflicting opinion. In brief, it refers to that process whereby the doctor *offers* the patient a new perspective on or new meaning to something the patient has presented, perhaps in the form of dreams, symptoms, feelings and behaviour. The doctor has therefore to avoid taking too much at face value. Rather, she examines material as it is presented (the 'manifest content') in an effort to find some underlying meaning (the 'latent content'). Sometimes, using interpretations the doctor will try to link together what to the patient seem to be unrelated and discontinuous ideas, feelings and events. This may be achieved, for instance, by helping the patient to integrate what goes on in therapy with what has happened in the past or what is happening in the present. 'It seems to me that your frequent silences suggest that you are angry with me because you feel as though I'm not giving you easy solutions to your problems. Perhaps that's something you have felt before in relationships?' The frequent focus on past events is not merely an empty biographical exercise. In a sense, the past is ever present because it continues to have an effect on how we structure our lives. We ought to be aware of this effect because, as Santayana, the American philosopher, has warned, 'Those who do not remember the past are condemned to relive it'; they 'act it out'. The past should not be a straitjacket and therefore many patients have to be freed from it.

Learning when, what and how to make interpretations is a skill that is not easily acquired, and students of psychotherapy often react in two entirely different ways. Some, impressed by the powerful effect of interpretation, strafe their patients with interpretations; but, as might be expected, poorly timed and insensitive interpretation will probably only jeopardise the therapeutic relationship, leaving patients more disturbed, hurt and confused than they were before therapy began. (Lomas (1987) has provided an instructive account of how interpretation may be abused.) At the other extreme, some therapists are too reluctant to interpret because they are not sure that their interpretations are 'correct'. This, however, is the wrong way to look at interpretations. The reality is that no therapist has been granted a gift of infallible observation and judgement, and therefore an interpretation has the status only of a hypothesis to be tested. Suggestions such as 'I wonder if you aren't feeling rather angry and fed up just now' are usually more appropriate than are bold statements such as 'You're feeling angry and fed up'. The doctor has to listen for themes and echoes and offer an interpretation to the patient as an alternative way of making sense of the patient's behaviour and experience. This requires psychotherapists to be able to tolerate ambiguity and uncertainty just as their patients have to do.

'Working through' is an equally important concept, although it has become a cliché. Correctly used, it applies to the inevitably time-consuming process of exploring and digesting new ideas, experiences and insights. To 'see ourselves as others see us' or to change our view of the world and to test out new ways of behaving are not easy tasks, because we need time to consolidate, monitor and adjust to these changes and their consequences, including the reactions of others. One particular change to which a patient may have to adapt is the loss of his symptoms. Not only do some symptoms provide the patient with 'primary gain' (by protecting him from emotional discomfort), they may also achieve 'secondary gain' either by evoking the sympathy and attention of other people, or by giving the patient a means of controlling his environment. It is not difficult to imagine, for example, how certain symptoms, such as headaches, frigidity and depression may create secondary gain for the patient by allowing the patient to be excused responsibilities or by ensuring that attention and sympathy is forthcoming. It is frequently the threatened loss of secondary gain that accounts for the resilience of symptoms despite heroic treatment efforts. Some patients do not enjoy good health!

There are two additional points to be noted. The first is that no matter how important the therapy is to the patient, the 'treatment hour' is but one twenty-fourth of the patient's day. Neither the patient nor the doctor can afford to ignore the realities of the patient's life, for the ultimate test of change and development is not how the patient fares in therapy, but how he or she deals with these realities. The second point is that no matter how skilled the doctor is in the use of the techniques and methods just described, she will make no progress unless she listens empathically to her patient. It is a pity that the capacity to listen is often undervalued among clinicians and students. Too much emphasis can be placed on doing something to or for patients. This may be one reason why, in the early stages of their training in psychodynamic therapy, doctors tend to ask too many questions, instead of adopting a rather more passive, listening role. This fault is particularly obvious with seriously ill or disabled patients. I recall once a patient with multiple sclerosis saying to me, 'I wish you doctors would stop telling me what can be done for me as I get worse, and listen to how I feel about things'.

What Problems or Patients can be Best Helped by this Therapy?

Now that we have covered some features of the theory, aims, methods and techniques of psychodynamic therapy, it will already be obvious that this form of therapy is not suitable for all patients. It is for this reason that the general question 'Does it work?' is a ridiculous one. If anybody asked, 'Do throat lozenges work?', it would not be possible to give an unqualified answer. They may be helpful for certain throat ailments, but they are not too useful if you happen to have a sexually transmitted disease!

Certainly, practitioners of psychodynamic therapy can draw comfort from the increasing body of evidence which testifies to the value of this particular treatment (e.g. Garfield and Bergin, 1986), but there are no grounds for complacency. For a variety of reasons, including theoretical, moral and economic ones, psychodynamic therapy must be subjected to critical and empirical scrutiny, along with other forms of medical treatment. At the same time, however, we must be wary of the possibility that, because verbal therapies often draw the heaviest fire from critics, double standards are not used such that these therapies are more rigorously examined than others (Shapiro and Shapiro, 1977). Moreover, whilst it is not acceptable for psychodynamic therapists to seek refuge in the claim that psychodynamic concepts are merely metaphors (Spence, 1988), it must be acknowledged that there are formidable obstacles facing those who wish to conduct properly controlled trials of treatment involving psychodynamic therapy. This point was forcibly made by the determined, but ultimately abortive, efforts of Candy et al. (1972) to carry out a controlled trial of three forms of psychotherapy, including dynamic therapy.

Although we need to know much more about what particular therapy, carried out by whom, under what conditions, works for which patients with what problems, there are already some useful guidelines (e.g. Bloch, 1979) that practitioners can follow.

First of all, with this form of therapy, little progress is likely to be made with patients who are in the grip of psychosis. Psychotic patients are so out of contact with reality that they find it almost impossible to engage in a realistic way with a psychotherapist (although see Chapter 4 and it is certainly worth reading Freeman's (1988) valiant and painstaking efforts to relieve the suffering caused by certain symptoms of schizophrenia). Secondly, patients of very limited intelligence and verbal fluency are not going to gain much from a therapy which is so evidently biased towards reasoning, understanding and verbal communication. (It is important, however, not to exaggerate such factors. Even patients of limited intelligence can be suitable for this therapy providing the doctor makes sufficient effort to explain things and work at a level consistent with the patient's abilities and experience.) Thirdly, although this is not a problem exclusive to psychodynamic therapy, patients who either have no real motivation to change or have grossly unrealistic expectations of therapy are not good prospects. Some patients are quite refractory to insight, and others see doctors as merchants of happiness who will provide them with a 'cure' and contentment without any effort on their own part. Fourthly, the doctor has a responsibility to ensure that the patients' personal, social and family resources would allow them to cope with the demands of therapy. Finally, patients who find it difficult to think in psychological terms, who are not at all introspective and unable to reflect candidly on themselves, are likely to find this form of therapy unrewarding and unnecessarily stressful.

As more experience is gained in using this form of treatment, doctors often find that more patients than expected turn out to be suitable. In any case, even if these guidelines are employed quite strictly, there is no shortage of patients to be helped. Patients with problems in relationships, neurotic disorders, grief reactions or disorders of personality, as well as those with psychosomatic disorders, can be regarded as possible candidates for psychodynamic therapy. With regard to the last group, it is revealing to note that anything between 30 per cent and 40 per cent of patients present to their family doctors with physical symptoms that have no detectable organic cause. To a large extent inspired by Balint's (1957) persuasive demonstrations of how patients cannot be thoroughly assessed and treated by general practitioners without some attention being paid to the doctor–patient relationship and to the psychological significance of the symptoms with which the patients present, there has been a growing awareness among doctors of the need to develop what might best be called 'psychodynamic awareness', i.e. a basic grasp of some of the fundamentals of the psychodynamic approach, as described above, can be helpful in most areas of medical care, including following trauma (Alexander, 1990), without the practitioners claiming to be or even wishing to be seen as 'psychotherapists'.

In deciding for or against the use of psychodynamic therapy, we should avoid being unduly influenced by the patient's clinical problem or diagnosis. Two patients with the same clinical picture will have their own constellation of relationships, their own personal view of life and their own attitudes to therapy and change. Moreover, helping patients in a dyadic relationship is only one way of using psychodynamic principles and techniques. For historical reasons, and for clarity of presentation, individual psychotherapy has been the focus of our attention, but these principles and techniques can also be used in working with couples, families and groups, as will be shown in Chapter 8.

Summary and Conclusions

As a means of alleviating a patient's distress, the distinctive feature of psychodynamic therapy is its focus on unconscious mental processes and events which are thought to underlie the patient's symptom or presenting problem. The therapeutic relationship is regarded as the critical element in therapy because it is in the context of this safe, caring but *professional* relationship that the patient can become aware of and explore the significance of this unconscious material.

The assumption that this form of therapy makes about human beings and their ills does not, however, deny the importance of other influences such as genetics, the environment and culture. It is also important to be aware that this mainly verbal form of therapy is not incompatible with other forms of treatment, such as medication or behaviour therapy, provided that there is a sound therapeutic rationale to the concurrent use of other forms of treatment. For instance, it is quite possible that very depressed patients might require a course of antidepressants in order that they can function at a level at which they could benefit from psychotherapy.

Classical psychoanalysis is undoubtedly the prototype of the numerous varieties of psychodynamic therapy which have emerged. Chapter 3 will consider some of these developments: some of these modifications have developed from the prototype, whereas others have probably appeared as a reaction against the original model. Theoretical as well as practical considerations have, for example, fostered a move towards briefer versions of this kind of therapy (see Bauer and Kobos, 1987; Sifneos, 1987). Sociocultural factors have probably also played a part in the shaping of new therapeutic approaches. For instance, Western society has changed since the early days of psychoanalysis from being highly authoritarian and rigidly hierarchical to being more democratic and egalitarian. Part of this change may be reflected in the therapeutic relationship which has developed from a benign but distant 'father–child' relationship into a more open and flexible one. Others have leavened the heavy psychoanalytical dough by the introduction of humour into therapy (Kuhlman, 1984). Another important change is that psychodynamic therapy is not used solely, as it was initially, to treat mental illness and relieve symptoms; instead it is often used to help people with 'problems of living'. The boundary between 'treatment' and 'personal growth' has now become extremely blurred.

To judge from its increasing popularity, it is obvious that psychodynamic therapy is a 'growth industry' but, regrettably, the evaluation of this form of therapy remains a 'cottage industry'. Perhaps the general issue of its effectiveness is no longer in doubt (Garfield and Bergin, 1986), but we still remain in relative ignorance about what the effective elements in the process of therapy are: more research is clearly required. In particular, there remains the challenging question of whether there are effective ingredients specific to psychodynamic therapy or whether these are 'non-specific factors' which Frank et al. (1978) claim to be the potent and ubiquitous influences in any effective form of psychotherapy. However, just because we do not yet have incontrovertible empirical support for our theories and techniques, we must not abandon them in despair. They are a genuine attempt to structure and make sense of what practitioners do and how patients respond. Until more data are available, all practitioners will have to act as their own 'researchers', looking candidly at their results and examining the assumptions which underlie their work. This will also require them to consider how to blend professional skills and knowledge together with personal qualities and the desire to care for a patient. Being merely 'caring and compassionate' is not enough (and, in any case, practitioners of psychotherapy have no monopoly on such qualities). Nonetheless, doctors must not let the technical aspects of the treatment stand in the way of what must be their primary task – the alleviation of suffering. The doctor faced with difficult clinical situations can be tempted to hide behind techniques, jargon and theories. Facile intellectualisations about the patient suffering from an 'unresolved oedipal conflict' may provide the insecure therapist with a spurious sense of understanding of his or her patient's problems, but such statements guarantee no relief of suffering for the patient.

References

ALEXANDER, D.A. (1990). Psychological intervention for victims and helpers after disasters. *British Journal of General Practice* 40, 345–348.

ALEXANDER, D.A. and EAGLES, J.M. (1990). Which neurotic patients are offered which psychotherapy? *British Journal of Psychotherapy* 6, 401–410.

ALEXANDER, D.A. and HALDANE, J.D. (1979). Medical education: a student perspective. *Medical Education* 13, 336–341.

ALEXANDER, D.A. and HALDANE, J.D. (1980). Medical education: the discontinuers' view. *Medical Education* 14, 16–22.

ALEXANDER, D.A. and RITCHIE, E. (1990). 'Stressors' and difficulties in dealing with the terminal patient. *Journal of Palliative Care* 6, 28–33.

BALINT, M. (1957) *The Doctor, His Patient and the Illness*. London: Pitman Medical.

BAUER, G.P. and KOBOS, J.C. (1987). *Brief Therapy: Short-Term Dynamic Intervention*. Northvale, NJ: Aaronson.

BERNE, E. (1966). *Games People Play*. London: Deutsch.

BLOCH, S. (1979). Assessment of patients for psychotherapy. *British Journal of Psychiatry* 135, 193–208.

BREUER, J. and FREUD, S. (1964). *Studies on Hysteria*, translated by J. Strachey. London: The Hogarth Press.

CANDY, J., BALFOUR, F.H.G., CAWLEY, R.H., HILDEBRAND, H.P., MALAN, D.H., MARKS, I.M. and WILSON, J. (1972). A feasibility study for a controlled trial of formal psychotherapy. *Psychological Medicine* **2**, 345–362.

ERIKSON, E.H. (1950). *Childhood and Society*. Norton, New York.

FRANK, J.D., HOEHN-SARIK, R., IMBER, B.L. and STONE, A.R. (1978). *Effective Ingredients of Successful Psychotherapy*. New York: Brunner/Mazel.

FREEMAN, T. (1988). *The Psychoanalyst in Psychiatry*. London: Karnac.

FREUD, A. (1936). *The Ego and the Mechanisms of Defence*. London: The Hogarth Press.

FREUD, S. (1960). *The Psychopathology of Everyday Life*, translated by J. Strachey. London: The Hogarth Press.

GARFIELD, S.L. and BERGIN, A.E. (1986). *Handbook of Psychotherapy and Behavior Change*, 3rd edn. New York: Wiley.

KRIS, A.O. (1987). *Free Association: Method and Process*. New Haven: Yale University Press.

KUHLMAN, T.L. (1984). *Humor and Psychotherapy*. Illinois: Dow Jones-Irwin.

LAKIN, M. (1988). *Ethical Issues in Psychotherapy*. Oxford: Oxford University Press.

LOMAS, P. (1987). *The Limits of Interpretation. What's Wrong with Psychoanalysis?* London: Penguin Books.

MACASKILL, N. (1988). Personal therapy in the training of the psychotherapist: is it effective? *British Journal of Psychotherapy* **4**, 219–226.

MAYS, D.T. and FRANKS, C.M. (1985). *Negative Outcome in Psychotherapy and What to Do about It*. New York: Springer.

MORENO, J.L. (1953). *Who Shall Survive?* New York: Beacon House.

NEMIROFF, R.A. and COLARUSSO, C.A. (1985). *The Race Against Time*. New York: Plenum Press.

SHAPIRO, D.A. and SHAPIRO, D. (1977). The 'double standard' in evaluation of psychotherapies. *Bulletin of the British Psychological Society* **30**, 209–210.

SIFNEOS, P.E. (1987). *Short-Term Dynamic Psychotherapy: Evaluation and Technique*, 2nd edn. New York: Plenum.

SPENCE, D. (1988). *The Freudian Metaphor: Towards Paradigm Change in Psychoanalysis*. New York: W.W. Norton.

SULLIVAN, H.S. (1953). *The Interpersonal Theory of Psychiatry*. London: Tavistock.

VAILLANT, G.E. (1986). *Empirical Studies of Ego Mechanisms of Defense*. New York: American Psychiatric Press.

WOLSTEIN, B. (1988). *Essential Papers on Countertransference*. New York: Columbia University Press.

Further Reading

BELLACK, L. (1981). *Crises and Special Problems in Psychoanalysis and Psychotherapy*. New York: Brunner/Mazel.

BROWN, J.A.C. (1961). *Freud and the Post-Freudians*. Harmondsworth: Penguin.

CLARK, R.W. (1980). *Freud: The Man and the Cause*. London: Weidenfeld and Nicolson.

ELLENBERGER, H.F. (1970). *The Discovery of the Unconscious*. London: Allen Lane.

ERIKSON, E.H. (1953). *The Interpersonal Theory of Psychiatry*. London: Tavistock.

FRANK, J.D. (1969). *Persuasion and Healing*. New York: Schocken Books.

GARFIELD, S.L. (1980). *Psychotherapy: An Eclectic Approach*. Chichester: Wiley–Interscience.

GLOVER, E. (1955). *The Technique of Psychoanalysis*. New York: International University Press.

GUNTRIP, H. (1977). *Psychoanalytic Theory, Therapy and Self*. London: Hogarth.

KOVEL, J. (1978). *A Complete Guide to Therapy*. Harmondsworth: Pelican.

MALAN, D. (1979). *Individual Psychotherapy and the Science of Psychodynamics*. Guildford: Butterworths.

RYCHLAK, J.F. (1973). *Introduction to Personality and Psychotherapy: A Theory–Construction Approach*. Boston: Houghton Mifflin Co.

STORR, A. (1979). *The Art of Psychotherapy*. London: Secker & Warburg and William Heinemann Medical.

SUTHERLAND, S. (1976). *Breakdown*. London: Weidenfeld & Nicolson.

SZASZ, T. (1979). *The Myth of Psychotherapy*. Oxford: Oxford University Press.

Chapter 3
Psychoanalysis: Departures from the Traditional Freudian Way

HAROLD MAXWELL

Classical theory, known also as drive or instinct theory, is described in the previous chapter. It proposes that the two drives of sexuality and aggression are inborn, and that frustration of their discharge leads to the developing individual experiencing 'unpleasure', whilst the eventual discharge evokes 'pleasure' or at least the end of 'unpleasure'. Classical analysts regarded the psychological problems of patients as conflicts between the id (infantile impulses pressing for discharge), being countered by the morality of the super-ego (conscience), and the defences of the ego (reality).

The fashioning of a concept of human beings which is reminiscent of the models that obtained in the physical sciences was obviously attractive to Freud, the natural scientist, but this approach was not so appealing to others. Indeed, theory development of this sort became a point of departure for at least two early and significant associates of Freud, namely Carl G. Jung (1875–1961) and Alfred Adler (1870–1937). Both of them became disenchanted with Freud's biological extrapolations and, in particular, with his emphasis on the sexual drive.

Jung produced an off-shoot school of his own with the title 'Analytical Psychology', concepts of which included *individuation*, i.e. the coming together of various aspects of the subject's personality, including his or her 'opposite-gender' characteristics. He used the term 'Animus' for the unconscious, masculine side of the woman's female persona and 'Anima' for the equivalent in the man. 'Persona' is the front we present to the world as opposed to the 'Shadow' which we keep hidden.

Other terms used by Jung (the Swiss-born psychiatrist) were: *personal* and *collective unconscious*, the latter referring to the myths common to all mankind; *extroversion/intraversion* which denotes whether an individual's instinctive life is mainly suppressed or overt; and *archetype* which is a symbol and part of the collective unconscious (Jung, 1968).

Adler also founded his own school, called 'Individual Psychology', which was concerned with a more social view of human beings, emphasising such things as the importance of birth order and sibling rivalry. He wrote also at length about the concept of inferiority, inventing the term 'inferiority complex'. The latter can be general or sometimes, according to Adler, concerned with specific body organs either in reality or in fantasy (there is a connection here with hypochondriasis and psychosomatic medicine). The individual strenuously attempts to compensate in all possible ways and strives to 'become somebody'. These efforts range from healthy adaptive ways to unpropitious neurotic, psychotic or antisocial ways. The concept of 'striving for power' is pertinent here (Adler, 1956).

Modern theories have continued this drift from the emphasis on the dynamic interplay between competing biological drives occurring within the individual. Successors to the early theorists argue that such notions, whilst not to be discounted entirely, are too simple and do not reflect the complexity and subtlety of human behaviour. Moreover, it might be argued that attempting to construe human behaviour in terms of 'forces', 'energies' and 'structures' sounds too much like a desperate but inappropriate effort to mimic the style of reasoning and theory development characteristic of the physical sciences.

An equally important fact, which has itself contributed to a revision of theory and practice, has been the nature of the problems and symptoms presented by patients. Nowadays, therapists are confronted with patients whose major concerns are not clearly defined symptoms, such as those with which Freud dealt, but rather a general dissatisfaction with themselves as people and/or with their interpersonal relationships. Bowlby's work on 'attachment behaviour' (Bowlby, 1979), the work of Mahler on separation–individuation (Mahler, 1967) and the efforts of the (British) *object relations* theorists, such as Fairbairn (1952), Winnicott (1958) and Balint (1968), are important examples of theoretical developments which reflect contemporary clinical problems. According to these theorists, the motivational drive in humans is to seek relationships with others, and the difficulties or, indeed, the successes, people have in this regard can usually be traced to the influence of very early experiences, particularly those between mother and child. In therapy, this line of reasoning focuses not just on the individual patient's symptoms, or even on the patient as an individual, but rather on the patient in the context of his or her relationship with others (Hamilton, 1988). This object–relations approach is also consistent with *systems theory*, which is closely linked with treatment of the family (Minuchin, 1974), and with the neo-Freudian schools of therapy, to which clinicians such as Horney (1939), Erikson (1950) and Sullivan (1955) contributed so much.

The work of Melanie Klein (Segal, 1964), which had its origins in child analysis, was largely developed in London, where it continues to have a very significant influence, and where trainee analysts, especially from Latin America, Spain and Italy, have come to study and later propagate her work in their own countries. In other parts of Europe and in the USA, her teachings are regarded with more reserve, although even in these places much of what she innovated is used and frequently quoted.

Klein thought that the ego, with all its instincts and anxieties, is present at birth, and described 'positions': the 'paranoid–schizoid', followed by the 'depressive' – both referring to anxieties suffered by the individual. The 'positions' recur throughout life, influenced by external and by innate factors (Klein especially emphasised the latter and many analysts have criticised her for this).

During the 'paranoid–schizoid' episodes, anxiety is predominantly for the self; 'splitting' and excessive projection are the main defences; when the, later, 'depressive position' is reached or reactivated, splitting is lessened, and a dim awareness begins – slowly and painfully – that goodness and badness can coexist within the same person (the mother and the individual himself).

Other Kleinian features include a strict technical adherence to the transference, close attention to projective and introjective mechanisms, and a literal acceptance of the death instinct which, so Kleinians believe, manifests itself as aggression and, particularly, envy.

Melanie Klein's teachings have stimulated interest in fields beyond psychoanalysis and psychiatry: educationalists and criminologists, and those concerned with aesthetics have found her work of value.

Another group of theorists, the ego analysts, who included Hartmann (1958) and Rapaport (1951), have also made a significant contribution to the understanding of human behaviour and experience, by directing attention to the way in which people guide, and are largely responsible for their own actions. The emphasis by these theorists on human 'self-determination' entailed an important shift in the view of mankind. Human beings are not being portrayed as hapless victims of irresistible and turbulent internal (intrapsychic) forces; instead, they are depicted as the major architect in the construction of their own present and future.

Despite these and other more recent developments, strong traces of traditional Freudian notions reappear, sometimes under a different guise. To some extent, this is the case with aspects of Berne's theory of transactional analysis (Berne, 1966), which is attractive, as it is readily understood by patients and professionals. One of the key concepts generated by this theory is that of the 'ego-states', of which Berne identified three: the 'child', the 'adult' and the 'parent'. The boundaries of these three are not hard and fast but, according to Berne, at different times one of these states may assume control, giving our behaviour and experience a characteristic 'flavour'. The 'parent' is similar to the more traditional idea of the super-ego, in that it refers to that part of our personality which reflects the ideals and moral values of the family and culture to which we belong. The 'child' makes its presence felt when, for instance, we 'let our hair down' and act on our more basic, egocentric and less socially acceptable impulses. Behaving in this way might also be described as allowing the id to assume control. The remaining ego-state, the 'adult', is that part of ourselves which allows us to deal rationally and maturely with our own internal needs. Again, the correspondence can be seen between this concept and the more traditional Freudian one – the ego.

One particular point, mentioned in Chapter 2, justifies repetition – the importance of *conflict*. Theories about human nature abound; some of them emphasise the physical and biological aspects, whilst others focus on the interpersonal and social influences. However, the linking theme of all these theories is that of the potential for and the importance of conflict – after all, the contribution of conflict to human diseases and dis-ease is a character-istic feature of psychodynamic theory and its therapeutic counterpart, psychoanalysis.

Modifications of the Transference

The unique characteristic of psychoanalysis is the concept of *transference*, the utilisation and 'working-through' of which, within the analytical situa-tion, provides a living experience, both cognitively and experientially.

In order to foster the transference by encouraging free-flowing and regressive fantasies, the analyst traditionally stays out of the patient's physical and emotional sight during the entire course of the treatment, whilst the patient lies on a couch and is invited to 'free associate' generally without interruptions, censure or judgement. But this technical measure of the anonymous analyst has been criticised by some writers (Ferenczi, 1932; Suttie, 1935; Lomas, 1987) and above all Kohut, who have suggested that the use of the transference, as outlined above, is often experienced by the patient as coldness and aloofness on the part of the analyst, and could repeat, in the consulting room, real experiences of rejection in the early environment. Such techniques, these and other authors believe, are the very antithesis of fostering, albeit implicitly, the love and respect for the patient which, it is suggested, is the only basis of success in any psychotherapeutic procedure, including psychoanalysis.

The above authors, whilst retaining the concept of 'transference', maintain that 'scientific' and detached interpretations may serve as a defence on the part of the analyst against sharing the patients' painful feelings. In other words, the analyst in this sense employs a stratagem which cannot succeed if the purpose of the therapy is the evolution of change or modification in the patient's state. Unlike other medical specialties, knowledge or information is not enough in this situation. The authors considered here attest their belief that, just like any other helper of a person in deep emotional distress, something more than the foregoing is necessary, and the conviction of Ferenczi that 'no analysis can succeed if we do not succeed in really loving the patient' is strongly supported. Ferenczi especially advocated a more open and spontaneous attitude, to the extent that, notwithstanding his position as perhaps the closest of the half a dozen original associates of Freud, the latter eventually virtually disowned him as a result of his innovative techniques, although to the end of his life Ferenczi himself maintained a loyalty and attachment to the psychoanalytical movement and to Freud.

In a neglected and greatly undervalued study, Suttie (1935) similarly described how he felt that the physician's reserve and aloofness resulted in a one-sided unresponsive love relationship which must evoke anxiety, inhibit feelings and spontaneity, and destroy the companionship for the patient which, Suttie felt, was the essence of psychotherapy; he castigated what he saw as the *taboo on tenderness* which he believed was countertherapeutic in this form of treatment. He never joined the psychoanalytical establishment.

Lomas (1987), who *was* formally trained, but has since resigned from the International Psychoanalytic Association, describes how his own style of working avoids what he sees as a detached insensitivity on the part of the therapist, which could bring about a repetition of earlier repressive and deprivation experiences. He favours a parenting role similar to that of Winnicott which he sees as humane, non-authoritarian, spontaneous and imaginative, and above all empathic.

Kohut (1971, 1984) and Winnicott (1958) continued to practise formal analysis; they worked within the transference and, unlike Suttie and Lomas, never subscribed to a 'cure-by-love' technique. However, in their own ways they concentrated on a style whereby early empathic breaches in the patient's life were hopefully repaired. Winnicott taught that the mother–child couple should be understood as a single unit, becoming the analyst–patient unit, as opposed to the two entities of mother *and* child (patient *and* analyst). Kohut developed this (empathy) concept as opposed to merely providing insight for the patient, and evolved what he called 'self-psychology'; this, like the foregoing, involves a degree of empathy rather more overt than in classical psychoanalysis. He believes that, when it becomes clear that there were *real* childhood deprivations, interpretations alone will not be sufficient to enable the individuals to progress or mature. Kohut felt that the provision for what was lacking in the earliest years must be provided by the analyst, especially in severe personality problems, and described 'special' transferences using himself as a mirror or a 'self-object', thereby allowing himself to help the patient affirm his or her identity and develop self-esteem. He did this by unconditionally accepting the patient as a person, without, however, condoning the negative or aggressive aspects of his character.

Secondly, he allowed the patient to experience him (the analyst), for a while, as a much needed wise and knowing figure with whom the patient could identify. Thirdly, he became a twin or alter-ego for the patient, something for which, many believe, there is a universal longing. Kohut thought that, in many instances, a real lack of experiences such as these in the earliest years could engender a life-long feeling of being unreal and undervalued, with the result that defences, symptoms and negative personality traits would evolve, often preventing a fulfilled life. The damage to the developing individual's self-esteem, in particular, would result in difficulties in future relationships, and in the negotiation of life's inevitable 'slings and arrows'.

By extrapolation from the analytical situation to real life, friends, colleagues and partners become mirrors affirming the individual's existence, and a career or leisure activity comes to represent expertise and knowledge, thereby enhancing self-respect and strengthening of the personality.

Evolution in the Aims of Psychoanalysis and Psychoanalytically Based Psychotherapy

Originally, as classical psychoanalysis was developing, it was felt to be essential and therapeutic that consciousness should replace that which is unconscious, largely using cognitive measures: ego (reality) replaced id (i.e. basic instincts). *Insight* was the goal, so that a more pragmatic approach to life generally was encouraged. Within the analytical situation, and again according to classical theorists, repressed sexual and aggressive impulses towards early 'objects', i.e. close members of the family (hence the incestuous connotation), were *transferred* to the relationship between the patient and the analyst, and hopefully resolved during the treatment. The focus of the therapy was to examine within the transference the defences that emerged, against the patient's unacceptable aggressive and sexual drives.

Kleinian analysts would see the aims of treatment as being the 'integration' of the personality: the patient gradually develops a diminished need to endlessly *project* his or her own bad traits into the environment. These practitioners feel that when any projection takes place, 'good' attributes as well as 'bad' are projected (lost) and impoverishment of the personality inevitably results. Others, already mentioned, believe that, for therapy to be successful, a modification of the technique employed by the traditional analyst should take place, because a detached technical attitude may merely replicate early rejecting experiences, so that a therapeutic impasse may be reached which is damaging and immutable. These authors 'show' themselves to a varying extent, and may openly convey empathy, so that which was not provided, and yet was so much needed in the earliest formative years of the patient (i.e. *the installation of unconditional acceptance and the building of self-esteem*), can have a second chance of being developed through the analysis. (See also Searles (1965) whose sparkling writing is devoted to describing a style of treatment in which the analyst fearlessly merges with the patient, even temporarily sharing some of his own psychotic processes, thereby countering the desperate isolation of the latter, and resulting in an unusual depth of understanding and prospect of change and development.)

In any event, what is becoming increasingly accepted is that, in the case of severely deprived and hence vulnerable individuals, something more than the traditional, anonymous model of the omniscient analyst is required. These patients, variously designated 'borderline', 'schizoid', 'narcissistic' or 'personality-disordered', seem to need more flexible technique and management.

When reading clinical accounts of these sobriquets, the doctor will recognise aspects of him- or herself at various times in his or her life, realising that, when considering human psychopathology, all is a matter of degree and threshold; there is no 'them' and no 'us'. As has already been noted, it is problems of everyday living, and particularly relationships, rather than florid psychiatric symptoms, that bring today's patient to the psychotherapist. In this regard, the latter should be especially alert to the emphasis and strength of 'narcissistic defences', such as splitting, denial, projective identification (see Chapter 1) and omnipotence. Characterological features in these patients include a great sensitivity to criticism, poor self-esteem, mood fluctuations, impulsiveness, volatility of mood, an ill-defined sense of personal and gender identity and frequent recourse to drug and alcohol abuse.

Narcissism and Narcissistic Disease

This is generally a pejorative term suggesting selfishness and egocentricity, but in the psychoanalytical sense it has come to be understood as a character-ological reaction to early deprivations, especially the failure of the establish-ment of an early and life-long self-esteem, due essentially to the lack of an unconditional acceptance by the mother. *It is today's greatest challenge to analytical psychotherapy, both in theory and in practice.*

As has been said, nowadays patients seeking help from an analyst or psychotherapist often tend to have vague and existential problems which, if sufficiently severe, can merit the accolade of a DSM III entry as 'narcissistic personality disorder', the features of which include: (1) a grandiose sense of self-importance; (2) preoccupation with grandiose fantasies; (3) exhibition-ism; (4) a sense of detachment and indifference to others but with the expectation of special favours – this is associated with rage, shame, poor self-esteem, emptiness and depression if criticised; and (5) interpersonal exploitation.

Summary

Some theoretical and practical 'advances' in traditional psychoanalysis have been sketched, but the overall goal is still an enhancement of the patient's self-esteem and independence, and an increase in his or her sense of trust and cohesion.

References

ADLER, A. (1956). *The Individual Psychology of Alfred Adler*. New York: Basic Books.
BALINT, M. (1968). *The Basic Fault*. London: Tavistock Publications.
BERNE, E. (1966). *Games People Play*. London: Deutsch.
BOWLBY, J. (1979). *The Making and Breaking of Affectional Bonds*. London: Tavistock Publications.
ERIKSON, E.H. (1950). *Childhood and Society*. New York: Norton.
FAIRBAIRN, W.R.D. (1952). *Psychoanalytic Studies of the Personality*. London: Routledge & Kegan Paul.
FERENCZI, S. (1932). *Clinical Diary*, edited by Judith Duport and translated by Michael Balint and Nicola Zarday Jackson (1988). Cambridge, MA: Harvard University Press.
HAMILTON, N.G. (1988). *Self and Others: Object Relations Theory in Practice*. New Jersey: Aaronson.
HARTMANN, H. (1958). *Ego Psychology and the Problem of Adaptation*. New York: International Universities Press.
HORNEY, K. (1930). *New Ways in Psychoanalysis*. New York: Norton.
JUNG, C. (1968). *Analytical Psychology: Its Theory and Practice*. London: Routledge & Kegan Paul.
KOHUT, H. (1971). *The Analysis of the Self*. London: The Hogarth Press.
KOHUT, H. (1984). *How Does Analysis Cure?* Hillsdale, NJ: Analytic Press.
LOMAS, P. (1987). *The Limits of Interpretation*. London: Penguin Books.
MAHLER, M. (1967). On human symbiosis and the vicissitudes of individuation. *Journal of the American Psychoanalytic Association* 15, 740–763.
MINUCHIN, S. (1964) *Families and Family Therapy*. Cambridge, MA: Harvard University Press.
RAPAPORT, D. (1951). *The Organization and Pathology of Thought*. New York: Columbia University Press.
SEARLES, H. (1965). *Collected Papers on Schizophrenia and Related Subjects*. London: The Hogarth Press.
SEGAL, H. (1964). *An Introduction to the Work of Melanie Klein*. London: Heinemann.
SULLIVAN, H.S. (1965). *The Interpersonal Theory of Psychiatry*. London: Tavistock Publications.
SUTTIE, I.D. (1935). *The Origins of Love and Hate*. London: Kegan Paul. Reprinted by Pelican Books, 1960.
WINNICOTT, D.W. (1958). *Collected Papers*. London: Tavistock Publications.

Chapter 4
The Trainee's Feelings and the Clinical Relationship

JON SKLAR

It is difficult to imagine a comprehensive medical training that does not include elements of the significance of mental factors in illness and its treatment. Yet such shortcomings in medical education may later result in the blindness of physicians not interested in the problems of human living, both healthy and diseased. It may also lead to the training of practitioners who are less than skilful in their handling of the doctor–patient relationship and of the process of healing.

In contemporary medical training there are usually courses on medical psychology, which often take place early in the curriculum and, when such teaching is based on academic or experimental psychology preoccupied with the measurement of detail, it cannot meet the requirements of students wishing to understand the doctor–patient relationship.

The problem for both doctors and patients is that being human they have, inevitably, a range and depth of emotions and feelings. This is often particularly charged in relation to the body and body-illness. People have emotions about the ill parts of their body, which constitute at base a 'phantasy' of the pathology. Knowing the truth usually helps to allay the fears regarding this phantasy. Of course, doctors themselves suffer from phantasies and medical students especially so. It is well known that the latter harbour at some time or another all the medical afflictions of their textbooks.

One vital aspect of *examining* patients is that emotions may be taken into account. They can be very involved and the doctor is often provoked to experience a whole range of feelings about the person he is invited to treat – these feelings include anger, common sympathy, caringness and antipathy. If the doctor is aware of them, they are much less likely to interfere with the communications with his patients, than if they remain unconscious.

The preoccupations of life may be said to be basically three-fold: birth, sexuality and death, and these three preoccupy the 'internal world' of the human being, especially the world of a growing infant. The medical student has often a great burden to bear during his or her studies; somehow, all that must be learnt about bodies – nakedness, genitalia, sexuality, birth and death – has to be integrated into the student's own perception.

What, for instance, is the emotional impact of one young person examining another young person's body? On the surface, this seems an irrelevant question and it is usually ignored in medical school. Yet the trainee enters medical school with various notions and phantasies about bodies, theirs and other people's. To the student preoccupied with keeping 'hands to oneself', the idea of touching another's naked body may be a source of acute embarrassment, almost as if it were a sexual advance. Somehow the student has to stumble through all the 'sexuality' of the meeting of the doctor and patient, in a state of mind which is usually unprepared and in an atmosphere where such aspects of medical training are vigorously ignored.

I remember witnessing the mixture of horror and excitement in a male colleague who during training was asked to examine a young man. The latter shook and reacted as if having orgasm as the student attempted to palpate the abdomen. The patient was deeply embarrassed by his discharge soiling the sheets and the student likewise did not finish the examination, let alone the clerking. Similarly, how many students can cope with the demands made by the necessity to examine the body of a patient as old as that of one's parents? It may be extremely hard at first for the student to bear to look at 'parents'' nakedness.

What is the trainee to do in such a bewildering 'sexual' world? The underlying theme of medical education is to harden the student's attitude. This is the right and proper direction. Who would want to be treated by a surgeon who had qualms about sticking a knife into another person's body or by a doctor who fainted at the sight of blood and mess? It is likely that the beginning of such a toughening up of the character armour begins in the dissecting room where medical education has usually commenced. This fact, in itself, is an indictment of medical education, where the process of making a doctor begins with an experience of a dead body rather than the birth of a baby.

Yet this desirable process of defending him- or herself against anxieties may become so exaggerated that the student builds such a tough armour around him- or herself that feelings never come to be acknowledged and the future doctor may then be left untouched by death and pain.

If this splitting process develops too far, it can become a pathological state. The adolescent patient in casualty who swallows two aspirins more than the proper dose, with the expectation of death, may be perceived by the hardened doctor as not worthy of his or her medical expertise. It is not a medical emergency in which a life can be saved and the patient is whisked out of casualty by the doctor, who is angry at having his or her time wasted. Yet for that patient, the experience of being close to death may have been very high and it has gone quite unnoticed by the closed mind of the doctor, interested only in the body and distanced from the pain in the patient's mental state.

How else may medical students cope with such assaults on their emotions? The common occurrence of both heavy drinking and excessive sexuality in an often closed hospital/institutional system may be considered as defences against the anxieties on the part of trainees and trainers in the course of medical education. Instead of pondering on themes such as, 'One day, will I be old and have such and such an awful pain?', anxiety is relieved by dissolving it in alcohol or the forgetfulness that goes with coitus.

Up to a point, this is the stuff of an undergraduate life, with its crises of maturation. Yet medical students devolve into doctors, many of whom retain these apparent coping mechanisms which can in extreme cases be taken to the excesses of alcoholism, drug addiction and ultimately suicide. It may be argued that such issues have little to do with medicine, but I think the seeds may well be laid down in undergraduate training for such pathological splitting processes to occur in later life.

One method of investigating the anxieties and feelings of the medical student in relation to the beginnings of his or her clinical work is within the context of the training seminar. The difficulty is that such doctor–patient skills cannot be taught: they can only be experienced. Such a seminar is a development of Michael Balint's studies with general practitioners (Balint et al., 1966) which in turn followed seminars with social workers dealing with marital difficulties. It became clear to Balint that ordinary didactic methods were of limited value, but if in the case discussion attention was focused on the development of the client–worker relationship, a considerable increase in the worker's understanding and effectiveness resulted.

Extrapolation to a medical student group, where clinical problems are brought, in which the student feels stuck and lost, can be equally illuminating. The seminar is concerned with the understanding of the student–patient relationship. The aim of the seminar is to develop in the student a sensitivity to the patients' emotional problems, thereby to enable the former to understand them more precisely and in greater depth, and to help him or her acquire skills and understanding for a greater therapeutic effect. To quote Balint: 'A pre-condition for the acquisition of this increased sensitivity is a general loosening up of the doctor's personality, especially with regard to his professional work. He must be able to notice and to tolerate emotional factors active in his patients that he rejected or ignored before and he must learn to accept them as worthy of his attention.'

Balint is discussing qualified doctors who have already acquired this professional armour. It is likely that medical students can benefit, by being invited not to don such protective measures so early in their training. The seminar technically compares a given individual's way of treating patients with those of his or her colleagues in the seminar. A group setting is used to demonstrate that any form of treatment entails a specific kind of interaction between the patient and the student doctor.

The realisation may dawn on the seminar, including its leader, that mistakes may be made. The discovery that *the* correct therapy for any given patient does not exist soon emerges. Instead, there are often several sensible directions to pursue, each of which has advantages and disadvantages. The student may choose one suitable to the relationship between the patient and him- or herself and acceptable to both. Part of the work is to acquire the capacity to think, to make hypotheses, test them and see the results. This is often seen by teachers as a vague area and is defended against, usually by the doctor taking up rigid attitudes to his or her work.

It can be very hard for the students to begin to find their place in the clinical scenario. Doctors, nurses and patients all have a seemingly well-defined role on the hospital stage. Students often feel that they are only a burden to the patients and staff, someone who is in the way. It is common for students to be concerned at over-exposing an ill person to yet another clerk or examination. Certainly this may be true when a patient is treated as a body with a particular pathology, the self that is someone with feelings and sensitivities to the medical process being ignored. Yet this common undervaluing by the students of themselves is erroneous. The patient often relishes the attendance of the student as the only one with whom he or she can actually talk. All the trained staff may appear to be, or actually are, too busy to spend time in thinking with the patient about what is happening. This is precisely the position of the student who is also trying to assimilate what is going on. This common interest may enable the patient to divulge a much richer tapestry of findings than the plain somatic component. Each patient has a story to tell, has feelings about what is happening and, especially, phantasies of what is inside his or her body and what will be its outcome.

The sensitive student may quickly find that he or she has become a repository of knowledge about the anxieties of the patient and how the problems began. He or she may have been told, for instance, of the elderly patient's concern for his dog, his only companion for many years. Dealing with such a 'tiny' human problem may lead to a great lessening of the patient's anxiety, increase the therapeutic alliance and substantially alter the patient's feelings about his doctor and his medical treatment. *Yet it needs to be listened to.* And the student must be able to speak up for the psychological aspects of the patient's hospitalisation.

A student may find that the man with a myocardial infarction had his chest pain immediately following a row with his wife. Further investigation of the social system will reveal a marriage full of fights, with the husband's comment to his wife, clutching his chest in pain, 'You'll be the death of me'. Thus, there is a social and human context to the pathology of the heart. It may be necessary for marital therapy to be prescribed, as much as physical treatment for the damaged heart, this specific symptom being a metaphor for the pain of love.

Another example would be the patient who is only able to talk of impending death with the student and not with other staff who may 'know' and who perhaps are unable to face the pain of such a discussion. Students may find themselves specifically caught by the patient in order to have an audience for his or her fears and preoccupations. The former may only have an imperfect knowledge of the medical position and yet he or she can contribute a great deal to the psychological needs of the patient at such times. This is a crucial period for the student who must take a personal decision about the psyche-soma. Will the student identify with the consultants and trained staff in seeing medicine as an emotionally detached issue, ignoring the psychic pain of the patient and passing by? The alternative is to begin to know that the patient is a human being with a history of life and feelings and anxieties about his or her present predicament which need to be taken into account. The argument usually runs that this 'soft-end' of medicine takes up too much time. Such a rationalisation is untrue. The point is that the patient can be regarded as invisible, the body being only the container of pathology and illness, or experienced as a human being. Often the student can learn to be really in touch with the patient, a process often shunned because the qualified doctor may not be able to face the depression, the consequences perhaps of failure of medicine and the pain of sharing knowledge about feelings of what is happening. Yet the very act of being touched by a patient psychologically and, in return, letting the patient know that his or her anxieties and affects are understood, constitutes the essence of the Art of Healing.

In further consideration of clinical relationships, the patient's emotional state can often affect the student or doctor. The former may experience relief at having been able to 'get rid of' some weighty and unpleasant thoughts which are instead transferred to 'the other', and may feel in good safe hands, with less need to worry about the fear of destruction, pain, loss of function and death. The student/doctor, however, is left to ponder on the truth of the clinical situation. Some, if not all, the anxiety can then be further projected into, for instance, 'the tests'. If everything has been carried out correctly (blood examination, X-rays etc.) then student/doctor cannot be blamed for the outcome. Further we are living in a world in which the blame by the patient, or even society, for the illness is being directed onto the shoulders of the medical profession in the form of litigation. In such states, it is often hard to hold onto the notion that nobody is to blame for a particular ailment. Yet much mental work may need to be done by the young doctor to avoid taking on a burden of fault. This is not the same as being a caring physician in the sense of having responsibility for the correct medical environment to care for the illness. The medical student who trains with her own burden of guilt (usually unconscious) in relation to her particular history, may indeed find herself taking on the burden of medical guilt. Care is required to recognise that what is being experienced is a projection – in other words differentiation must be made from the patient. Superficially, this sounds somewhat facile, and yet many of us enter the medical profession in a state of unconscious confusion and uncertainty about our own state of 'illness'. Better in that case to be the doctor, the leader, the one who 'makes it all better', than the victim, the person who is ill. What comes to mind is the well-known dictum 'Physician heal thyself'. This, too, is a subtle projection of the illness phantasy of the doctor onto the patient. It is quite common to find, in the history of the student/young doctor, that illness in a sibling, parent or relative has had a profound influence from early years. The child witnessing the stress and dis-ease of illness in the family may rush to accept responsibility, and an unconscious desire is born to make it all better. Medicine is thus a useful career concept to locate such a desire. There is nothing wrong with such reasons fuelling the wish to be a doctor and the wise physician may well have some knowledge of it.

An example was the young doctor who, when she was six, watched the death of a 2-year-old brother with appendicitis, when the family was living for several years in a medically primitive part of India. It was clear at the time that her brother's death could have been prevented. The guilt that she was alive and he was not induced an extraordinary epistemophilic instinct to learn about illness and medicine. It is easy to imagine that the path is open to a state of depression when it dawns on the student, or later the young doctor, that medical knowledge and technology now cannot make up for the loss of the brother many years before. If not understood, this could lead, in time, to a disenchantment with medicine as a profession.

Another phantasy would be to cut off from the emotional pain in the patient as a protective device against re-experiencing an unresolved catastrophic pain in the early life of the doctor. Such a doctor would appear to be emotionally hard and apparently uncaring to the feelings of the patient and yet, beneath such a façade, there could exist a sensitive or even an over-sensitive awareness of pain, of illness, destruction and death.

Often a critical issue of being a doctor, which is rooted in childhood, is the capacity to work alone or with a team. Many doctors' character formations lead them to strive to be the hero, single-handedly combating the dragon of illness. Yet the more mature physician will know the enormous part played by the nurse. Nursing is an indivisible part of healing. The student may well observe the consultant appearing in the hospital ward for a small amount of time in the week. Much action occurs on such occasion: high-powered discussions, medications written up, procedures undergone, yet most of the time the patient is in the hands (literally) of the nurse. This part of the healing is underestimated by the student at his or her peril. The underlying psychology is the *need* of the baby to have two parents with different functions. Father is necessary to inseminate, but mother carries the fetus in her womb.

Mother suckles the baby but, in the best of worlds, is herself looked after by the father.

A similar analogy can be applied to the hospital wards. Doctors are essential to initiate the procedures directed towards cure, but it is the body of the patient in the hands of the nurse that enables the treatment to be satisfactorily applied. It is the combination of the doctor and the nurse which makes for good healing practice on the wards, be it general or psychiatric. These are matters for the medical student to observe in order to make sense of the medical relationships. The author is proposing a wider field of view than the apparently more simple one of unconsciously identifying with the consultant, i.e. copying the model presented to the students. This is a hard task because the fear of illness, and the fear of performing a medical procedure that may turn into an attack on the patient leading to death, make it more likely that the student will place omniscience and magical powers on the consultant–teacher than that he or she will identify with the healer in reality and without magical thinking. 'If I am like the consultant then I am not a danger to the patient.' Confirmation of the terror of causing injury to the patient can be seen in those many student colleagues who have to overcome what seems to be a huge resistance to taking blood from the vein of the patient.

Having mentioned death at various points, it would now be pertinent to consider the concept further in relation to the student, who is nearer one end than the other of life's journey. The heroic student, perhaps as a defence against the concept of his or her own death, may wish to do everything possible to sustain life. An alternative view would be to place the healing apparatus at the service of the dying patient in order to allow the process of death to arrive in as good a way as possible; after all it is one of the very few inevitable facts following birth. The quality of a person's life is arguably a more critical factor than mere length. It takes a maturity to judge what are often fine balances in this area, and the student should be under no illusion that such matters are in the hands of only the senior staff. It is usual practice for the junior houseman to decide to resuscitate or not. It is even more difficult to be in touch with the dying patient who may require frank discussion on time left in order to prepare for death. This task, which can be regarded as an essential one for the doctor in relation to the good care of his or her patient, requires a student to be aware of his or her own mortality. This needs to be struggled with inside each of us, but its resolution will enable the doctor to face what seems to be the unacceptable for some patients, and also for many members of the medical profession itself.

Reference

BALINT, M., BALINT, E., GOSLING, R. et al. (1966). *The Study of Doctors*. Mind and Medicine Monographs Series. London: Tavistock Publications.

Chapter 5
Psychotherapy in Liaison Psychiatry

CHRIS THOMAS

Introduction

Liaison psychiatry is a fairly recent term for a relatively old concept (Lipowski, 1974). It can be described as the activities carried out by a psychiatrist when working in the non-psychiatric departments of a general hospital. Usually, this involves the psychiatrist with patients who are suffering, or appear to be suffering, from physical illnesses. The term 'liaison' implies that a major aspect of this work is for the psychiatrist to share his or her findings, opinions and therapeutic suggestions with the medical and nursing staff who are primarily involved in managing the patient (Lipowski, 1981). Psychiatrists may offer their services in one of two ways (White, 1990): first, they can provide a consultation service which allows them to become involved with a specific psychiatric problem whenever a referral is made by a colleague. Once this problem has been dealt with the psychiatrist has no further contact with the referring department until the next problem arises. In a consultation service psychiatric referral is therefore always determined by the physician. As it is known that physicians may miss emotional problems (Maguire et al., 1974) or be reluctant to refer (Mayou and Smith, 1986), there is a risk that some patients who might benefit will not be seen by a psychiatrist. The other service is a more intense form of contact when a psychiatrist may be attached to another hospital department attending ward rounds, outpatients and clinical or teaching meetings. This liaison style allows regular contact between physicians and psychiatrists with the ability to share views and ideas over a variety of different clinical problems. It also gives the psychiatrists themselves the opportunity to initiate contact with a patient if they feel it appropriate, thus overcoming the problem of the physician failing to recognise a potential psychiatric problem.

It is becoming increasingly apparent that the purely biological approach to medicine is not sufficient and, to understand any patient fully, a wider perspective must be adopted which involves consideration of emotional and environmental factors, as well as physical aspects (Engel, 1977). New terms such as 'holistic medicine' or the 'biopsychosocial model' are being used to describe an approach to patient care whose origin goes back to Ancient Greece. These views perhaps tended to be overlooked in the last 100 years when, in a new scientific age, the biological aspects of disease undoubtedly took many steps forward. Now, however, awareness is returning that not all aspects of illness can be explained biologically and that both the causes and results of illness are multifactorial (Figure 5.1).

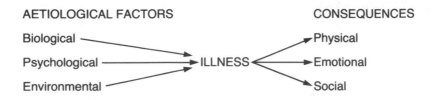

Figure 5.1 Aetiological causes and consequences of illness

It could be argued that, if patients should be viewed with this multi-factorial approach, then it would be wrong to have a psychiatrist involved with the psychological and emotional factors and that any doctor should be able to deal with all aspects. In the majority of cases, this should apply and only in occasional situations would a psychiatrist be needed, when psycho-logical considerations are particularly great and the doctor managing the patient may feel that he does not have sufficient knowledge or skills himself.

A liaison psychiatrist may become involved in many different problems that occur in general hospital patients, including organic cerebral states, self-poisoning, eating disorders, hysterical conversion states and abnormal illness behaviours (Gomez, 1981; Thomas, 1983). All of these problems may also present to a general psychiatrist and do not require different knowledge or skills from those already outlined in this book. There is one aspect of liaison psychiatry, however, which constitutes a major source of referrals, does not often present to a general psychiatrist and may require different skills. This is the area of psychological reactions to physical illness and the rest of this chapter will concentrate on these and how they may be helped through psychotherapy.

Therapeutic Needs of Liaison Psychiatry

If liaison psychiatrists are to deal effectively with the wide range of problems that is referred to them, then they will need a variety of different diagnostic and therapeutic skills (Lipowski, 1974). If they are firmly entrenched in either a pharmacological, behavioural or psychotherapeutic model of treat-ment, then there are likely to be a number of patients who will not benefit from referral. With each patient, the liaison psychiatrist must decide whether treatment will be most effective by using drugs, behavioural techniques, psychotherapy or, perhaps most commonly, a combination of these therapies.

Psychotherapeutic skills will undoubtedly be needed by the liaison psychiatrist and it would not be unreasonable to suggest that psychotherapy will be needed in varying degrees at some stage in the management of all his or her referrals (Thomas, 1985). In liaison psychiatry, psychotherapy can be used at three different levels: the psychotherapeutically oriented interview, supportive psychotherapy and insight-oriented psychotherapy. These different levels use different techniques and are employed to achieve different goals. There is no reason with general medical patients why a psychotherapeutically oriented interview cannot be used by any doctor without any specialised training, and supportive psychotherapy can be undertaken by most doctors after acquiring some basic skills. Insight-oriented psychotherapy, however, can usually only be used in general medicine by staff such as psychiatrists who have had specialised training and will not often be utilised by the medical staff themselves.

The basic goal of a normal clinical interview with a medical patient is to enable the doctor to obtain enough information to help him or her arrive at a diagnosis and plan the management. It is therefore a process largely for the benefit of the doctor. The psychotherapeutically oriented interview is designed as a modification of the usual clinical history-taking, whereby not only the doctor, but also the patient, benefit from the interaction. It is the goal of not only obtaining information, but also of feeding information back and establishing a rapport and a therapeutic alliance. At the end of the interview, the doctor will not only know about the illness, but will also know the patient and the way he feels about his problems; the patient will feel not only diagnosed, but also understood. Many doctors will claim that this is not psychotherapy but just good clinical practice which they exercise all the time. It is psychotherapy, albeit in a simple form, because during the interview the doctor will explore feelings, beliefs and attitudes and may outline to the patient certain features in his personality and background that explain why symptoms or illnesses have developed. The patient hopefully will be able to use this information in a constructive way to help him understand more about himself and perhaps even make some changes in his feelings or behaviour that lead to some relief of physical symptoms. Even in a single interview, a patient may feel accepted and valued by a doctor who shows an empathic awareness of his problems. If this occurs, the patient is more likely to feel safe about discussing fears and anxieties and, if these can be verbalised at the time, he may begin to evaluate them and obtain a sense of relief. The psychotherapeutically oriented interview can occur on every occasion that a doctor sees the patient and it does not require a set number of sessions. Indeed, it can often be used successfully with just one meeting.

In liaison psychiatry, supportive psychotherapy is often considered useful. Physical illness often represents a crisis and, not surprisingly, emotional health may be affected. In acute illnesses, patients may require emotional support from other people, either until recovery or until death. If the illness is chronic, or its consequences permanent, then support may be needed over a much longer period until acceptance of the illness has occurred. The skills needed are a development of these used in the psycho-therapeutically oriented interview and, providing they are willing to give the time, there is no reason why the vast majority of doctors should not be able to offer supportive psychotherapy to their patients. During this form of psychotherapy, the doctor is not concerned with factual information about the illness but concentrates on listening to the patient talking about the problems and, especially, about the fears and consequences of the illness. Helping the patient verbalise these is the doctor's main task. This process continues over a number of sessions rather than just a single interview, so that the patient can continue to build up a trust in the doctor, allowing them both to explore issues that may have remained hidden in early interviews. As well as verbalisation of feelings, the doctor should help the patient explore ways in which the problems and emotions can be dealt with more effectively. In many situations, it may not only be the patient who requires supportive psychotherapy: physical illness affects the whole family and all members may suffer and require support from medical staff. Also, in certain medical units, the pressures on staff may be enormous, due to the exacting and emotionally harrowing nature of their work. Consideration may therefore need to be given to the provision of support to the staff on these units.

Dynamic psychotherapy is intended to help people come to understand, and eventually change, certain aspects of themselves by the gradual uncover-ing of unconscious motivations and defences and potentially it is of great use, at least in some of its aspects, in managing patients with physical illness. In some people, the reactions to physical illness may seem exaggerated or even quite different from those normally shown by patients with the disease. These atypical reactions may be a result of unconscious factors in the patient, rather than a pure response to the stress of the disease process and then psychotherapy may require dynamic as well as supportive approaches to help the patient change to a more normal emotional response. Dynamic psychotherapy may be time-consuming, requiring many sessions, and its use will thus be restricted; part of a liaison psychiatrist's job will be to assess which patients may benefit most from dynamic therapy and to concentrate on offering it effectively to such patients.

Psychological Reactions to Physical Illness

All patients have feelings and thoughts about their disease and treatment and therefore all illnesses will be associated with various psychological reactions.

Many reactions will be minor, but in a few instances there may be a severe reaction that causes problems in its own right, separate from the physical distress of the illness itself. Sometimes, the reaction produces a problem which affects relatives or hospital staff more than the patient him- or herself. The severity of the psychological reaction is usually dependent on how threatening the illness is perceived to be. This, in turn, will depend on factors in three areas: the disease itself, the person concerned and the situation produced. Certain illnesses are commonly perceived as being threatening to the sufferer, particularly those where the patient believes there is a risk of death, severe disability, prolonged pain, a mutilating outcome or unpleasant treatment. Severe psychological reactions are therefore not infrequent in illnesses such as cancer (Maguire, 1985), myocardial infarction (Mayou et al., 1978), renal failure (Salmons and Blainey, 1982), chronic degenerative disorders (Earll, 1986) and especially when patients know they have a terminal illness of whatever course (Stedeford and Bloch, 1979). As well as factors in the disease itself, the threat of an illness will be influenced by aspects of the person suffering it. The various reactions that a given patient has developed in the past for dealing with stress will play an important part in shaping his or her psychological reaction to illness. A person who believes she has control over situations may develop a more positive, 'fighting' approach to serious illness which will help lower distress, whereas someone who feels she has no power to deal with stresful situations and is in the hands of fate may suffer severe emotional disturbance with the same illness. The previous awareness the patient has of the disease will also affect response. In psychotherapy, with the physically ill, it is therefore essential that the doctor explores the background, attitudes and beliefs of the patients as well as knowledge about how they have coped with illnesses and other stresses in the past. The other factors which determine the threat of the illness, apart from those of the disease and the sufferer, will depend on the situation that may result from it. Certain illnesses may not in themselves be threatening, but may nevertheless interfere considerably with the patient's ability to perform normal roles and relationships. The financial, occupational, leisure, marital, sexual and parental consequences may be more distressing than the physical effects of the illness. A man may tolerate an epileptic fit itself, but if his job had depended on a car, then the loss of his licence will cause major problems

Case 1   Mr H.M.

This 47-year-old man had suffered a myocardial infarct 9 months previously. He was referred to the liaison psychiatry service as he had not returned to work and, in the absence of continued cardiac disease, he complained of chest pain, palpitations and other symptoms. It was felt that this man was suffering from a severe anxiety state that was producing his symptoms. The patient readily accepted that his excessive worry over his health was associated with the knowledge that his brother had died at work shortly after returning following a heart attack. The patient's personal knowledge of heart attacks was therefore of a poor prognosis and consequently very frightening.

Psychotherapy with the physically ill will require the exploration of all the factors that may play a part in shaping the psychological response. It is of great importance that the therapist does not start with preconceived ideas about the stresses that the patient suffers.

At the beginning of therapy it is essential to make a full assessment of all the stresses the patient has to face with his or her illness. Different patients with the same disease process may have quite separate problems to face and therefore it must be up to them to decide which stresses need dealing with, rather than for the therapist to assume which ones are present.

Among the difficulties to be faced may be the problem of uncertainty as to whether the illness will get better or not; for some patients it can be almost intolerable to know that even after treatment there is a possibility that the illness may recur at a later date. Obviously a major stress for many people will be the knowledge that their illness may well end in death; this will be associated with many feelings associated with a sense of failure, incompleted life tasks or unattained goals and sometimes loss of spiritual faith. Other patients may dread certain physical symptoms such as pain or vomiting that may be associated with their illness. The sense of helplessness and need to be dependent on other people again may be very hard to bear, as may also the fear of being isolated or rejected by others because of their illness. With some patients it may be the treatment that produces more stress than the illness itself. Certain surgical procedures may cause body image disturbance (such as mastectomy and colostomy), and some modern chemotherapy regimes can produce prolonged and extremely unpleasant physical side effects. This list of possible stresses is far from complete and it cannot be emphasised enough that the therapist must allow the patient the opportunity to outline his or her particular stresses.

The form of the psychological response to a threatening illness will, in many patients, be a mood disturbance such as anxiety and depression. However, in some, the psychological reaction will be exhibited as a defence mechanism that the patient utilises to reduce the potential mood disturbance (Figure 5.2).

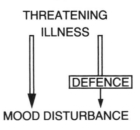

THREATENING
ILLNESS

DEFENCE

MOOD DISTURBANCE

Figure 5.2   Psychological response to a threatening illness

The psychotherapist will soon need to gauge the severity of any mood disturbance and to decide which, if any, of the defences the patient is using. He or she will also have to decide whether the defence is effective and should be encouraged, or whether it is causing problems that are worse than the mood disturbance it tries to prevent and, therefore, should be tackled through psychotherapy.

Anxiety and Depression

The majority of patients with a threatening illness will at some stage show evidence of anxiety or depression, and this is usually quite understandable and does not require specific psychiatric intervention. Anxiety results from uncertainty, whereas depression is the result of unpleasant knowledge. Many illnesses carry both uncertainty and unpleasant facts and most patients show features of both mood disturbances. Nevertheless, it is unreasonable to assume that because it is 'normal' it does not require attention. The attention it requires is in the form of supportive psychotherapy which can be carried out by any doctor, nurse or even student and may not require much time.

The first part of the psychotherapeutic management is to recognise the distress. This involves not only direct questions about mood, but also observing and commenting on non-verbal responses of the patient that indicate underlying disturbances. In some patients it may be appropriate actually to suggest that they should feel upset, if it appears as though they are hiding their feelings, and such a comment might release a considerable amount of pent-up emotion.

The therapist should then allow the patient time to talk about all his fears and depressive feelings without too many interruptions. The simple procedure of allowing patients the chance and time to 'get problems off their chest' is a very powerful aid in supportive psychotherapy. Following this, the therapist should try to explain the reactions the patient is having in terms of what she knows about the illness and the person; again, it can be very reassuring for a patient to have his mood disturbance understood by another person. The patient should be helped to realise that he is not alone in his feelings, that others have felt the same and he is not unusual or mad. Usually associated with this understanding is an implied permission that he is allowed to feel the way he does. Occasionally, patients think they are not allowed to be upset and believe medical staff would be angry if they openly showed emotions (unfortunately, they are sometimes correct in this belief). In psychotherapy, 'permission' is given for the patient to be open about his feelings to himself as well as to the therapist. The patient should also be given permission to continue to feel distressed and know that the therapist realises the stresses will be present for some time and that talking about them does not make them disappear. Thus the therapist conveys to the patient her acceptance of his feelings in an uncritical manner. In further sessions, the therapist may feel disappointed that the patient appears to go over the same ground continually, but in supportive psychotherapy this is often important. By repeated talking about stresses and release of associated emotions, the patient gradually adapts and the depression and anxiety diminish. To aid this process, it is occasionally useful to encourage the patient to share his feelings with other people, especially his family. In lengthy illnesses, the therapist will also help the patient look at stresses that may arise in the future, so they can be worked on and sorted out before they give rise to emotional disturbance.

A few patients will have mood disturbances that are less understandable in that they are very severe or last longer than usual and may require more specialised attention (Maguire, 1985). Sometimes, they can be helped with supportive psychotherapy and the addition of psychotropic drugs or behavioural techniques, but others may require more intensive dynamic psychotherapy. This more intensive psychotherapy helps the patient explore underlying reasons for an excessive reaction. Patients sometimes believe that they are responsible for their illnesses and occasionally view the illness as a justified punishment for past failings. This leads them to believe the illness is deserved and their prolonged depression becomes a form of penance. Other patients may, through their own illness, re-experience the feelings and emotions that were associated with the ill health and death of other people, such as parents, and their prolonged depression can be understood as a form of delayed grief. Sometimes, a severe or lengthy mood disturbance is the result of feelings that their life has been wasted and they have unfulfilled ambitions and dreams that will never come to fruition. All these sorts of problems may require delicate handling in a more protracted psychotherapeutic relationship.

> *Case 2   Mrs R.L.*
> A 53-year-old woman had undergone treatment for cervical cancer. She remained severely depressed and suicidal for several months. During psychotherapy it became apparent that she had been sexually abused by her father during childhood. She had harboured a deep-seated guilt over this, believing (quite unfairly) that she had been responsible. Her cervical cancer became, in her own eyes, the punishment to her sexuality that she felt she deserved. Over a number of sessions these beliefs were gradually explored and altered allowing her to lose some of her guilt and become less depressed.

Denial

Denial is oten the first reaction a patient shows when he or she first has to face a threatening illness. Providing it does not last too long, it is a normal and understandable defence that prevents the patient from being flooded with severe emotions at a stage when he or she is not yet ready to deal with them. Denial can be used both against facts and also against the emotions associated with the facts. Initially, the patient may deny the diagnosis or its seriousness. He or she may believe the doctors are wrong and this occasionally leads the patient into not believing the medical staff and into requesting a second opinion. This denial of facts does not usually last for more than 2–3 weeks but is occasionally accompanied by a longer denial of feelings when the patient accepts his or her diagnosis, but reports a state of numbness or emotional emptiness. During this phase, he or she has great difficulty in experiencing the appropriate degree of depression or anxiety that the illness would be expected to produce.

Over time, the numbness gradually reduces, to be replaced by understandable depression and anxiety. Denial in this sense is therefore a useful and necessary defence allowing the patient a period of time to accept gradually the situation he or she is faced with and to find other defences to cope with the psychological distress. This early and relatively short-lived denial should therefore not be removed psychotherapeutically and it would be cruel to make the patient face facts and emotions before he or she is ready. The medical staff should gently present the facts as they know them to the patients and allow them to question them. It is important that, if the patient appears to disbelieve or want another opinion, the doctor should not feel that this is a personal attack and therefore become angry, but should understand the patient's need to assimilate the information slowly as the denial decreases.

In some patients, denial may last much longer and become a very poor defence. In these cases, the patients may refuse to believe that their illness is serious or even that it is present at all, and this may prevent them complying with therapy and occasionally even stop them seeing doctors at all, which obviously puts them at risk. It is important in these instances to try and gently penetrate the denial, using psychotherapy, so that the patient accepts correct treatment. Even if the patient allows the medical team to carry out treatment, denial over a long period may cause hardship to a family, as the patient will be prevented from perhaps making necessary arrangements, in case the illness becomes terminal. It may also prevent the family talking with the patient over important issues that they feel need to be discussed. In these cases, if the family wish it, psychotherapy may be needed to help the patient drop the denial. It is not unusual for patients using denial to show periods of considerable anxiety or depression. This would seem to indicate that it is not a consistently effective coping strategy at preventing psychological distress and again, in these circumstances, it would be appropriate for the therapist to try and gradually persuade the patient to stop denying and to face the real emotions. If the denial, however, is not interfering with treatment or upsetting the family, then the therapist must seriously consider whether it is best left untouched if it is successfully preventing anxiety and depression, and allowing the patient to cope.

Case 3 Mrs J.B.

This 64-year-old lady was sent to a hospice with widespread bony metastases from a breast cancer. Although she had been informed of the diagnosis she consistently refused to accept it. She claimed that the problems were due to arthritis and that the doctors and nurses were incompetent for not being able to recognise this. She refused all offers of palliative help and insisted on taking her discharge from the hospice and returning home. She was seen by a psychiatrist regularly but continued to maintain her denial of her illness and eventually died some weeks later at home without ever accepting any help.

It is also important to realise that some terminal or chronic patients have fully come to terms with their illnesses and disabilities and have decided not to talk about them and to live the rest of their lives without continually being concerned about their health. This may at first appear to be denial, but obviously is not and it would be inappropriate to try to alter this form of coping through psychotherapy.

Anger

Another common reaction to serious illness is anger, which may first appear when denial fades. During this phase, the patient tries to find someone or something to blame for her predicament. Often, the blame will be levelled at the medical or nursing staff, who may be accused quite unfairly of missing the diagnosis, delaying treatment or purposefully providing false information. At the same time, close relatives and friends may be criticised and told that the illness is their fault because of past stresses they have subjected the patient to. Some people turn their anger towards God for allowing the illness to fall upon them. Even strangers can be blamed for being well, whilst the patient suffers and a frequent complaint at this time is, 'Why me?'. This anger is again an understandable defence when the patient is slowly becoming aware of the full facts of her diagnosis and prognosis. It gives the patient a sense of unfairness but provides her with an aggressive, fighting attitude rather than allowing her to sink into a state of hopelessness and inactive depression.

In the majority of people, it does not last too long and one of the main tasks of a therapist will be to help other staff and relatives understand the process and to reassure them that it will pass and the patients will not carry grievances for the rest of their lives. It is important that those involved with the patient listen to his or her anger and empathise with him or her, without actually agreeing that people have been at fault. While listening, alternative explanations can be offered if the patient has misconceptions about the causes or management of the illness, but outright arguing with the patient should be avoided as this will lead to confrontation which may seem to confirm the belief that others have wronged him or her. It may be possible to get the patient to shift the aggressive attitude away from other people onto the actual disease process itself and this may help him or her develop a positive approach with a belief of being able to fight and thus overcome the illness. Patients who develop this fighting spirit towards the illness usually manage to cope well from a psychological view point.

Unfortunately, in a small number of seriously ill people, anger becomes a fixed defence leading to a permanent sense of unfairness and aggression towards others. This tends to lead to major breakdowns in the relationships between the patient and his medical carers, his relatives and his friends and they may become permanently isolated. It is tragic when a person dies alone because all his contacts have been driven from him by his chronic anger and, if this seems to be occurring, it is a very deserving situation for a psychotherapeutic approach. The therapist must show the patient that he can accept his anger and then try to persuade him to look at the feelings it is preventing. This ultimately involves the therapist in exploring the underlying depression and anxiety and perhaps helps the patient to cry and be despairing. Hopefully, with psychotherapy, the severity of the depression can be worked through so that the patient gradually accepts both the illness and the people who wish to be close to him while he is ill. Sometimes psychotherapy reveals that the purpose of anger is actually to drive someone very close away from the patient, so as to prevent him from being hurt. The patient may believe that if he antagonises a relative prior to his death, the relative will not suffer in the bereavement. The patient needs help to realise that this is rarely successful because usually the relative will grieve even more if they have not been close together in the final stages of the illness. In these situations the therapist may need to work with both patient and relative.

Case 4   Mr S.S.

A 34-year-old man with severe multiple sclerosis was referred to the liaison psychiatry service because of abusiveness and irritability that was causing severe marital problems. After a number of stormy sessions when the psychiatrist frequently became the focus for the patient's angry feelings, he began to gradually become less irritable but more depressed. The sadness was largely related to his increasing incapacity that had culminated in him needing a wheelchair. This decrease in his abilities occurred while his two sons became more physically active and much of his frustration had been due to his perceived loss of parental role related to his inability to join in. As the anger changed to sadness through psychotherapy, he was able to discuss his feelings with his wife and sons and, although still in the wheelchair, he discovered that his children still needed him as a father in many non-physical ways.

Independence and Dependence

In many patients there is a desire to remain independent as far as possible and only to use the services of the hospital when it is essential; this reaction is usually encouraged. Occasionally, a patient's independence may become out of proportion and, as with denial, may lead to rejecting perhaps vital treatment. A patient may, for example, refuse analgesics even though she is in pain. Sometimes, independence in hospital leads to subjects failing to cooperate with the routine most patients accept as a necessary part of the smooth running of the ward. Patients with heart disease may continue to smoke, or diabetic patients repeatedly to ignore their dietary restrictions. Independence can lead patients to reject offers of aid from family or friends and they struggle on, coping less and less but refusing to allow anyone to help. This behaviour is very distressing for the families who see the people developing more and more problems but not letting them become involved.

Psychotherapy will often be needed when independence is quite out of proportion to the situation. In some patients the problem can be resolved by helping to show them that allowing others to help is not a sign of weakness or 'giving in' to the illness. Occasionally, the problem is due to longstanding beliefs, and intensive insight-oriented psychotherapy may reveal that they are people who have never allowed anyone to control them and have always fought against authority. These patients need help to see that treatment is not a conflict situation between them and the doctors, but a joint effort on both sides to combat the illness.

Dependence is the opposite reaction to independence and occurs when patients allow the hospital or family to take over all aspects of their illness and take no personal control of it themselves. They will show no effort really to fight the disease and may show poor cooperation with all attempts at rehabilitation. It may get so severe that the patient remains bed-bound, becomes incontinent and requires feeding by others, without adequate physical reasons. This form of reaction in patients may be an attempt to protect themselves from underlying emotions by allowing other people to be responsible for the illness and therefore letting them do the worrying. As with independence, some patients show a habitual pattern of responding this way. In the past, whenever problems occurred, they regressed to the position of being a child and this allowed others to act in a parental way. Such people may never have become fully independent of their parents and may require detailed psychotherapy.

In physical illness, therefore, successful coping allows a patient to be independent in many areas of his or her life, but can also allow him or her to depend on others when the need arises.

Acting Out

Many patients deal with the anxiety of their illness by obtaining attention and sympathy from others. A few people find it too anxiety provoking for others to concentrate on their illness and may try to obtain the equivalent degree of attention by utilising highly abnormal behaviour patterns. This is known as acting out. It may involve excessive use of drink or drugs, lying, destructive acts, criminality or promiscuous behaviour. As the hospital staff or family will find these behaviours quite unacceptable, they will attempt to control them and it is while they impose the control that the patient will obtain the attention, even though it may be in the form of 'punishment'. These forms of behaviour will, therefore, change the whole focus of attention of both the patient and his or her attendants away from the physical disease onto the abnormal activity and reduce the anxiety of being ill.

Psychotherapy is usually urgently needed in these cases to prevent severe deterioration of relationships between the patient and the medical team. The staff should have the patient's behaviour explained to them and be advised that if attention is not given to the maladaptive behaviour it will tend to diminish. With the patient, the therapist will try to establish a relationship which provides the attention he or she is seeking, and then to explore gradually the real anxieties and concerns that the illness imposes. This may in some cases be exceedingly difficult, as the patient ultimately destroys all attempts by the therapist to engage in a proper relationship.

Over-confiding and Over-involvement

A common way of dealing with any stress is to gather knowledge about the problem and to discuss it with others to see whether solutions can be found. All patients use this method to at least some extent. In a few, this may be taken to extreme levels and become harmful. The patient may read many books about his disease and often concentrates on the worst interpretation. By questioning many members of staff he will normally obtain slightly different information from each one and then he becomes concerned about what he considers to be major discrepancies and assumes that something is being hidden from him. This process, rather than lowering anxiety and depression, may actually increase it.

Similarly, the patients may seek many people in whom to confide and continuously seek reassurance from them. Again, discrepancies may heighten psychological distress. Whereas relatives or friends are usually happy to listen to problems for a certain period of time, they expect that eventually the patient will adjust and talk less of his illness and more about other matters. If the patient over-confides, he may actually drive the person away and start to experience antagonism and rejection, which leads to more, rather than less, psychological disturbance.

In these cases, psychotherapy needs to be quite directive in preventing patients seeking information from many places and one person (preferably a senior member of the medical team) should be identified as the only source. The psychotherapist will usually allow herself to be the one person who will counsel the patient and help him work through his anxieties so that he does not need continual reassurance from other people.

Displacement

Another method by which anxiety may be dealt with is to remove it from its real source and transfer it to some other concern. A patient using this defence, called displacement, may deny any anxieties about his real illness, but become preoccupied with another body part, a non-illness-related situation, or even another person. A person with cancer may claim he has fully come to terms with it, but may continually complain of pain in another site for which no organic pathology is found. Alternatively, he may become extremely preoccupied with a minor stress at work or in a relationship that previously would not have worried him. Perhaps the most common form of displacement is when the patient starts to worry about other people, often complaining that it is the relatives who need help to come to term with the illness, not herself. In hospital, patients may displace their anxieties by making unwarranted accusations that the staff have mishandled or ignored another patient. They may try to help all the other patients and even try to usurp the nursing and medical staff by taking on their functions. These patients then become very hurt when the staff try to curb their excessive over-concern with the other patients.

Some patients may join self-help groups and use their displacement to become counsellors themselves. Patients who have genuinely come to terms with their illness may be extremely useful in counselling others with the same problem, but if the feelings have not been worked through and helping others is due to displacement of the counsellors' own anxiety, then they usually become over-involved with the person they are trying to help, lose objectively and cause more harm than good.

Psychotherapy is difficult to carry out with these patients because they refuse to admit any anxieties about their own illness and insist that the problems lie elsewhere. If they can be engaged in a relationship, the therapist has to try gradually to persuade the patients to examine the real underlying concern about their illness and more appropriately replace the displaced anxiety, and then to work with them in dealing with it more appropriately.

Case 5   Mrs J.L.

This 54-year-old lady had undergone mastectomy surgery 4 years previously for breast cancer. For 2 years she had been working as a voluntary counsellor for patients recently diagnosed with breast cancer. It became apparent to other people in the counselling agency that she was not always helping her clients as she frequently contacted their doctors and complained about the treatment they were receiving, claiming that her own experience gave her the knowledge of what was best for them. She upset a number of the women she was meant to help, who until contact with her had not been in any way unhappy with their treatment. It was suggested that the woman receive some counselling herself but she refused and she had to be asked to leave the counselling agency. Although impossible to be certain, it is highly likely that she had displaced some of her own anxieties about her illness onto other women with the same diagnosis.

Conclusion

The majority of people who have to experience a serious illness during their lives are likely at some stage to show one or more of the reactions described in this chapter. All patients, therefore, require psychotherapeutic support and understanding, though in the vast majority of cases this can be adequately provided by their own families and their normal medical attendants. Only occasionally will a liaison psychiatrist be required to carry out more intensive psychotherapeutic treatment.

Hopefully, the majority of patients will eventually come to some degree of acceptance of their illness and many will adopt coping strategies and defences that are entirely successful and will never require any intervention and for this reason they have not been mentioned in the chapter.

If all patients with physical disease are considered from the physical, psychological and social viewpoint at the same time, then it is probable that there will be a much higher degree of satisfaction in the treatment and care that they receive while in the hands of doctors and other medical staff.

References

EARLL, L. (1986). Psychological care of the chronically physically ill. *British Journal of Hospital Medicine* 1, 46–49.

ENGEL, G.L. (1977). The need for a new medical model: a challenge for biomedicine. *Science* 196, 129–136.

GOMEZ, J. (1981). Liaison psychiatry. *British Journal of Hospital Medicine* 9, 242–246.

LIPOWSKI, Z.J. (1974). Consultation–liaison psychiatry: an overview. *American Journal of Psychiatry* **131**, 623–630.

LIPOWSKI, Z.J. (1981). Liaison psychiatry, liaison nursing and behavioural medicine. *Comprehensive Psychiatry* **22**, 554–561.

MAGUIRE, G.P. (1985). The psychological impact of cancer. *British Journal of Hospital Medicine* **8**, 100–103.

MAGUIRE, G.P., JULIER, D.L., HAWTON, K.E. and BANCROFT, J.H.J. (1974). Psychiatric morbidity and referrals on two general medical wards. *British Medical Journal* **1**, 268–270.

MAYOU, R., FOSTER, A. and WILLIAMSON, B. (1978). Psychosocial adjustment in patients one year after myocardial infarction. *Journal of Psychosomatic Research* **22**, 447–453.

MAYOU, R. and SMITH, E.B.O. (1986). Hospital doctors management of psychological problems. *British Journal of Psychiatry* **148**, 194–197.

SALMONS, P. and BLAINEY, J. (1982). Psychiatric aspects of chronic renal failure. In: F. Creed and J. Pfeffer (eds), *Medicine and Psychiatry: A Practical Approach*. London: Pitman.

STEDEFORD, A. and BLOCH, S. (1979). The psychiatrist in the terminal care unit. *British Journal of Psychiatry* **135**, 1–6.

THOMAS, C.J. (1983). Referrals to a British liaison psychiatry service. *Health Trends* **15**, 61–64.

THOMAS, C.J. (1985). Establishing liaison psychiatric services – a personal view. *International Journal of Social Psychiatry* **31**, 149–155.

WHITE, A. (1990). Styles of liaison psychiatry: discussion paper. *Journal of the Royal Society of Medicine* **83**, 506–508.

Further Reading

CREED, F. and PFEFFER, J. (1982). *Medicine and Psychiatry: A Practical Approach*. London: Pitman.

LACEY, J.H. and BURNS, T. (1989). *Psychological Management of the Physically Ill*. London: Churchill-Livingstone.

NICHOLS, K.A. (1984). *Psychological Care in Physical Illness*. London: Croom Helm.

STEDEFORD, A. (1984). *Facing Death – Patients, Families and Professionals*. London: William Heinemann.

Addendum I: Liaison Psychiatry and Parasuicide – A Bridge

HAROLD MAXWELL

Although the exact figure is not known, an estimated number of 100 000 are thought to take a deliberate overdosage of drugs per year (Jones, 1977). This and other self-destructive acts constitute by far the most common emergency the psychiatric profession is called upon to deal with, usually by colleagues in the casualty and general medical wards. It is an 'unpopular' emergency with both medical and nursing staff, but can provide an opportunity, if approached with thought and understanding, of gaining an unusual degree of rapport with the patient, sometimes through a single session, or it may be the start of an extended therapeutic contract, a turning point in the patient's life.

As opposed to successful suicide, the condition most often occurs in females aged between 15 and 30 years, as a reaction to a loss or disappointment. Its frequent incidence should, far from evoking a sense of exasperation as Dr Hale's exposition highlights, illuminate the dynamics of the interaction between patient and doctor, so that the possibility of *emergency psychotherapy* may be initiated.

Reference

JONES, D.I.R. (1977). Self-poisoning with drugs – the past 20 years in Sheffield. *British Medical Journal* 1, 28–29.

Addendum II: Psychotherapy in the Management of Attempted Suicide

ROBERT HALE

It is hard to underestimate the value of the proper management of a suicide attempt. Even if he or she survives, it is a situation that offers the possibility of the patient either returning to the same vicious circle whence he or she came, or of helping him or her to move forward to something new. Whether or not the patient ends up in formal psychotherapy, the dynamics of this management have to bear careful study.

Many suicide attempts go undetected; the patient merely 'sleeps it off'. Sometimes relatives will allow this to happen. Their indifference may betoken their underlying animosity to the patient. When a GP is called, even he or she too may decide that nothing needs to be done.

For the most part, however, the patient is referred to a casualty department where, with the exception of violent alcoholics, attempted suicides are among the least popular patients. Medical procedures, some of which are of very doubtful value, are accompanied by such comments as 'Why didn't you

* This is an extract from *Psychotherapy in Psychiatric Practice* (1991) edited by J. Holmes, published by Churchill-Livingstone and printed with the permission of the publishers.

do it properly?' or 'Don't you think we have got better things to do with our time?'. It is easy to condemn these attitudes, but in reality they represent a natural response to the patient's aggressive act. Some regard these procedures, particularly stomach wash-out, as a potential deterrent to future attempts, and certainly they are experienced by the patient as painful and humiliating, but it is doubtful if they do deter.

A patient was reminded of a statement he made when he took a previous overdose that he would not do it again because he could not stand a stomach wash-out. He was asked whether these thoughts went through his mind when taking the current overdose. His reply was that his intention had been that there would not be a wash-out this time. More importantly, the stomach wash-out is an attempt by the staff to regain control of the patient's body, a control which the patient has taken from the medical profession in swallowing the tablets which usually his or her doctor had prescribed.

Where there is a medical reason for the patient to be admitted he is fortunate. Having attacked his body, to be allowed, forced even, to regress, and to have bodily needs placed first, may well be psychologically exactly what he needs. The hospital can act as a relatively neutral container for all of the patient's projections. What the patient does not need is contempt or disdain from the professional staff, hard as this is to avoid. Thus, supporting the staff of the acute medical wards who are dealing with suicide is an important part of the psychiatrist's work. Unfortunately, many patients are discharged or encouraged to take their own discharge without any psychological assessment, even though the latter is recommended by the Department of Health.

The assessment of the patient should take place as soon as possible after the patient has regained consciousness, because it offers an opportunity to begin therapy. If the therapist can be included in the original chaos and receives the basic raw projections immediately after the suicidal person regains consciousness, the need to repeat the suicidal act may be reduced. Once the process of repression and denial has started (possibly after the first night's dreamwork has been done), it will be necessary for the patient to recreate the same relationship with the same vulnerability to suicide. Delay in identifying and owning suicide fantasies allows old defences to be re-erected with the psychiatrist as an accomplice. As one woman put it: 'It is as though it was another woman who tried to kill herself last week'.

The assessment itself must have the following aims:

1. The identification of organic or floridly psychotic illness in order to arrange appropriate treatment.
2. To let patients know that the therapist takes their actions seriously, even if they do not.
3. To establish the extent to which the patient can look inwards at the reasons for his or her actions. Surprisingly, this is often much easier for

the patient in the disturbed state of mind immediately following a suicide attempt.

4. To encourage the patient to keep this access to unconscious processes open by offering both tentative interpretations and assuming that the patient will want psychotherapy. If the latter turns out not to be the case little has been lost.

5. If possible patients should not be returned to the same relationship from which they came. It is far safer to hand the patient over to the care of a willing neutral relative or friend. It is essential to impress upon this person the seriousness of what has happened. If no such suitable person can be found, it will be necessary to admit the patient to a psychiatric ward until such time as therapist and patient feel it is safe to let him or her return to the partner or to living on his or her own. The general principle as always must be that the supportive matrix is sufficient to contain the patient's pathology.

Therapy should start as soon as possible. The appointment must be within a period of time that the patient can manage. It is crucial that the therapist stays alive in the patient's mind. In this acute phase the promise of a session in 2 days may mean never, i.e. too long for the patient to hold the therapist in his or her thinking. A central belief of suicidal people is that they have the capacity to kill off all of their good objects. To offer them an appointment beyond their own timespan or with a person whom they have not met will be perceived as both a further rejection and confirmation of their belief of their own destructiveness.

Chapter 6
Psychotherapy in General Practice

ANDREW ELDER

'Hearing secret harmonies' (Anthony Powell)

The Setting

Specialised psychotherapy is concerned with the treatment of selected patients in a highly organised setting. The treatment of patients in general practice is very different; the surgery doors open onto the everyday world. In general practice the doctor is not set at such a careful distance, monitoring the various aspects of transference and projection, but enmeshed, a fellow traveller, more involved with his or her patients and their illnesses. It is High Street medicine. This difference gives rise to many of the difficulties of the setting, but also to some of its unique advantages for psychotherapeutic work. In general practice, the doctor is not concerned with the application of any particular therapeutic philosophy, but with whatever psychotherapeutic use he can make of the opportunities that arise as part of his everyday work. He is an *opportunist*. He carries with him whatever skills and awareness he possesses in whatever he is called on to do – visiting a dying patient at home, dealing with a 'minor' illness in the surgery, responding to an emotional crisis, or a problem concealed in a 'While I'm here, Doctor'. The general practitioner's psychotherapy is dressed in ordinary clothing.

Psychoanalytical theory gives us an essentially developmental view of human life, placing 'each individual in his own unique cultural and developmental context' (Brown and Pedder, 1979) and lays great emphasis on the quality of the human relationships that enable the individual's development from the earliest moments of life. Difficulties and conflicts, as well as satisfactions and achievements, are constantly present and may build up in such a way that a crisis or an illness develops. For a few patients this may lead to formal psychotherapy, but for the overwhelming majority it is neither sought nor appropriate. The doctor in general practice, however, is often already present at first hand, helping his or her patients with many of these experiences that are some of the psychological determinants of people's lives: the problems of birth and early childhood, sexual development and marriage, illnesses, death and losses of one sort or another. Morbidity and presentations to the doctor are known to increase when people are negotiating these major transitions of life, or life events. This means that the doctor is often involved when psychic history is being made. He can therefore influence this process, a little, both for better and for worse.

Listening

In this chapter listening and hearing are often referred to when the need for doctors to 'listen' to their patients and 'hear' what they are saying is being described. This does not mean a passive process of sitting back and listening to someone talk. It refers to the quality and intensity of the listening to feelings that lie behind the patient's words, and the sensitivity with which things are heard that the patient is only half saying. This requires considerable attention to detail: how the patient looks and behaves, his mood, what words he chooses, when he falters and changes tack and what is left unsaid; it involves respecting the patient's need to express emotion in his own way and hearing what thoughts and feelings all these things, and many more, elicit in the doctor's own mind.

Most communication from which something new may be learnt by the person communicating exists in a half-lit world of things that are only 'almost known' to that person. This is true of the patient communicating to his or her doctor and also true of doctors when they attempt any change in their understanding of their patients or their involvement with them. Both worlds, the patient's and the doctor's, are changing. It is the relationship between the two, referred to in this chapter as the doctor–patient relationship, that is of central importance.

Incidence

It is a commonplace that the incidence of emotional or psychiatric disorders seen in general practice is high. Figures vary widely; the problems of definition are great and the diagnoses made in general practice consultations depend as much on the doctor's own characteristics and attitudes, as on the patient's presentation. In a practice with a special interest in psychological disorders, 43 per cent of all patients seen had symptoms which were regarded as being of emotional origin; 11 per cent suffered from formal psychiatric illnesses and 32 per cent from a variety of stress disorders (Hopkins, 1956). In another survey (Goldberg and Blackwell, 1970), a general practitioner, who was again described as having a particular interest in psychiatric disorders, only recorded an incidence of 20 per cent of consecutive attenders as having evidence of psychiatric morbidity. It may be that another doctor, steadfastly physical in his or her approach and determined not to notice his or her patients' emotional problems, could achieve a significantly lower incidence still. Doctors are as variable as their patients.

Despite these differences in the doctors' diagnostic thresholds, it seems that the average general practitioner in this country is likely to have a significant number of his or her consultations, probably averaging around 30 per cent (Royal College of General Practiners, 1981) with people who have been propelled towards the surgery by apparent psychiatric symptomatology of one sort or another. This figure may rise to 60 per cent or more if consultations are included in which the doctor feels there is a significant element of emotional difficulty being presented.

Some people consult their general practitioners much more often than others. Approximately 50 per cent of the general practitioner's workload is generated by 10 per cent of his or her patients (Jarman, B., Constantinidou, M., Elder A.H. et al., 1985, personal communication). The members of each doctor's 10 per cent group may have more psychological characteristics in common with each other than with less frequently consulting patients who may, nevertheless, belong to the same diagnostic category (for instance, migraine, dysmenorrhoea or depression). Among the population who do not go to the doctor often are individuals who have similar symptoms to those who do (Miller et al., 1976). It is not the possession of the symptom or the disorder that characterises the patients who more frequently come to the surgery, but the fact that they come, whilst others do not. This realisation is vital to the general practitioner's work.

What Kind of Diagnosis?

Although the results of these surveys give us something of a statistical background to the general practitioner's work, they do so in misleading terms. Diagnoses of this sort belong to a psychiatric classification derived from what is often called the medical model. The doctor presides, uninvolved with his or her patient, and diagnoses the patient's illness according to certain symptoms and signs. Such a model encourages the doctor to think only about making the 'right' diagnosis and not about the patient, and inclines both the patient and the doctor to define the problem outside themselves, thus discouraging the doctor from thinking about his or her relationship with the patient. It is a model much used in hospital thinking, but it transfers very uneasily into general practice, where the emphasis is shifted more to people and away from illnesses; more to a longer-term perspective than to a two-dimensional view at one moment. It makes little sense to place two totally different consultations with people of different personalities and back-grounds with different problems and expectations into a single category called, say, anxiety state.

> A large woman in her sixties, who always has a timid look about her, comes to see the doctor about her painful neck which prevents her from sleeping. She is a bit overweight, tends to visit the doctor about once a month and is recently retired from her work as a cleaner. She comes to ask for a repeat of her arthritis tablets and wonders if her blood pressure is up (which it is, slightly). She cries when the doctor asks about her brother whom he knows she has been worried about and who is now dying of cancer. She is single, rather shy and has always felt large and awkward. She has remained closely attached to her large number of brothers and sisters since their father died when she was nine. They mostly live a long way from her and she is constantly anxious about them. The doctor has got to know her and how she uses him. He is happy to see her and takes her blood pressure, listens to her and prescribes more tablets. The consultation lasts ten minutes and will be repeated many times, in one form or another, as it already has been in the past.

Such a consultation is very typical of a general practitioner's work. Which diagnosis is the doctor to choose? Even sticking to traditional medical diagnoses, it would be difficult to choose between obesity, mild hypertension, cervical spondylosis, anxiety or depression. All play a part.

If we shift the emphasis from the medical diagnosis towards a more personal one, we immediately begin to include some life history, any important recent events, present tensions with other people and something of the patient's relationship to herself: her self-esteem and confidence, and her capacity for change and adaptation. These things may help us learn more about her emotional needs and what she may require from a visit to the doctor. The single page becomes biography.

It does, however, still leave out any account of the doctor's own particular viewpoint. The importance of this omission increases as the patient's subjective world is taken more into account. The diagnosis has to broaden again to include something of the doctor's own reactions and how he or she sees the patient. Today's view may be different tomorrow and the same patient would be seen differently by different doctors.

Knocking on the Doctor's Door

Among the sea of people who come in and out of a doctor's surgery, some people will have a relatively clear idea of why they have come and what they can reasonably hope to gain. Others are propelled by a less well-differentiated urge, a more generalised need for understanding or help, which they initially transmit to the doctor through their symptoms. These may resolve quite quickly or continue until the doctor and patient eventually settle on a distance and a language that is acceptable to both of them. This is then the 'illness'. It is particularly important for the doctor in general practice to tolerate uncertainty and not organise the patient's illness too soon. He or she may otherwise prevent important developments from emerging and contribute to what Illich has called the 'medicalisation of life'. The ground-swell of need which brings people to doctors is present in everyone. For some, it is more successfully met in life relationships than for others. The doctor is a relatively freely available figure. Maybe in previous times, such a need sought its expression elsewhere, through the church or within the extended family, but in today's world it knocks on the doctor's door. Both the patient and the doctor contain numerous possibilities for the outcome of their consultation together. They each have the potential for many different directions and levels of contact with each other. Nothing is static. Patients alter their patterns to fit their doctors and seek out doctors who reflect their needs. For many patients it may be more important that there is a channel of communication open to them when they need it, rather than its particular medical content.

Doctors develop different ways of responding to this challenge. Each doctor's own approach may be valid for himself. There is a risk in too great a conformity. If a doctor does decide to undergo appropriate training and learn to make himself more accessible to his patient's emotional needs, he must first become aware of the history and development of the thought that has already gone into trying to understand the nature of the general practice setting for this kind of work.

History

The history of psychotherapy in general practice is essentially the history of the impact of two psychoanalysts, Michael and Enid Balint, and their work with general practitioners. The story begins with general practice at a low ebb in the early 1950s, very much the junior partner within the medical profession. There was 'widespread dissatisfaction amongst general practitioners' (Collings, 1950) who at that time lacked any specific training for their work. The mismatch between the skills acquired through under-graduate medical training and those needed by the general practitioner in his or her work was even more acute then than it is now. Apart from their heavily disease-centred training, those doctors had mainly their commonsense and endless outpatient referrals to help them through.

In 1948 at the Tavistock Clinic in London, Enid Balint began leading a group of non-medical workers who were working with people having marital difficulties. Michael Balint, a Hungarian psychoanalyst whose father had been a family doctor, became interested in applying this method to study the difficulties general practitioners were having and to see if new techniques could be developed to help them in their work. In 1954, and 1955, the first reports of this work were published (Balint, 1954, 1955). It initiated far-reaching changes in the ways doctors and patients were subsequently to relate to each other. Much was learnt from his early work and was eventually published in 1957 as *The Doctor, His Patient and the Illness* (Balint, 1957), one of the masterpieces of medical literature.

From the beginning, this work was a marriage between the psychoanalytical background of the Balints and the medical work and attitudes brought to the groups by those first general practitioners.

The Balints contributed the setting, the aims, the open-mindedness of their enquiry and a belief in the value of human beings (doctors as well as patients). They also contributed their understanding of the unconscious and a basic trust that, from the ruminations of the doctors themselves, new patterns would emerge. They were non-moralising and non-didactic. They did not attempt to instruct the doctors in psychoanalytical theory or give them psychodynamic explanations of their patients' behaviour, or of the doctors' own behaviour for that matter. Through their own listening skills, enhanced by psychoanalytical training, they helped the doctors listen better to their patients. Winnicott and others have shown how a mother can respond more sensitively to her child if she has herself received what he called 'good-enough mothering' (Winnicott, 1972). By the same token, doctors are better able to respond to their patients' problems if they have had the experience of being listened to sensitively themselves in their training. They are then able to learn more from the main source and stimulus to education for doctors, i.e. *the patients themselves.*

The doctors also had much to contribute. They brought their openness and willingness to learn, which is never an easy process, and their preparedness to stick at a difficult task for a considerable length of time. They required what Balint came to call the 'courage of their stupidity' (Balint, 1957). This meant being prepared to use their minds imaginatively and contribute freely to the thinking of the group – not being too cautious and correct. This courage remains the main driving force for any group.

Training

The method of work and its aims have remained essentially the same over the years. A small group of general practitioners meet each week with a suitably trained leader and present cases that are giving them difficulty. They do so without notes which enables the doctor to give a more spontaneous presentation, disclosing to the group some of his or her own subjective reactions to the patient. With the help of the leader(s), the group then examines the doctor's and the patient's interactions over the whole of their relationship, and also focusing on the detail of a recent consultation: 'Why did you do that?', 'How did she react?', 'I feel that by prescribing for her at that moment, you were dismissing her', 'I don't think this patient can get through to you', 'I think you were caught in a difficult situation' etc.

> The doctor comes to the group with the real burden of a difficult case. In reporting his case and joining in the discussion, he tests his own ideas against those of this colleagues. In a way, the reporting doctor takes on the role of his own patient, and the group becomes the doctor. They share his anxieties and may pick up what he has missed due to his blind spots.   (C. Gill, 1985, personal communication)

The group process does not teach skills or manoeuvres, but aims at a 'limited but considerable change' (Balint, 1957) in the doctor's personality. It helps each participant to extend her range and methods of working by enabling her to use her own personal potential more fully. She gains additional understanding of her involvement with the patient and, over the years, gains a greater understanding of herself too.

There are many aspects of a doctor's work. It is the *integration* of these various elements and their appropriate use that is the aim of successful training. If the training results in a doctor who carries on his general practice regardless, but performs what might be described as 'psychotherapy on Sundays', it has failed. And if it results in a doctor who becomes so interested in pursuing his patients' psyches that he persecutes them with inappropriate curiosity, e.g. 'How's your sex life?', and becomes dissatisfied and neglectful of the rest of his medical work, then again the training has failed. A successful marriage produces a new individual, not just a chip off one or other of the old parental blocks.

It is the leader's job to preserve the aims of the group and help it remain focused on its primary task. Groups often prefer to do almost anything other than this. They take refuge by flight into other preoccupations and the leader has to watch out for these, steering a course between anecdotal chit-chat, journeys of psychological speculation into the patient's past, constant questioning of the presenting doctor or drowning him or her with 'helpful' advice, at the same time avoiding anything that might be too personal or painful for the doctor.

This method is both a technique for training, still remaining the principal one for training general practitioners in this sort of work, and a technique for research. For research it can be used to study the present state of play in the general practitioner's world, like a sampling net lowered at a particular point to chart the changes and developments that are occurring as the wider medical and social culture evolves. Some groups have also met to research particular aspects of their work, such as marital problems (Courtenay, 1968), repeat prescriptions (Balint et al., 1970) or abortions (Tunnadine and Green, 1978).

Developments

An important change of emphasis and technique occurred in the 1970s. During the early years, the doctors tended to become semi-psychotherapists, devoting long sessions to their patients with psychological problems. This was an inevitable side effect of the training and reflected the doctors' need to model themselves on the work of the leaders, a defence against the real difficulty of achieving an independent and appropriate professional identity for themselves.

The doctors' psychotherapeutic work had to become better integrated with their everyday work, making it less of a foreign body. New techniques had to be discovered to fit the general practitioner's timescale. A research group, again with the Balints' leadership, began meeting in 1965 to study this problem. They published their findings in a book called *Six Minutes for the Patient* (Balint and Norell, 1973). The change in thinking that lay behind this work was as significant as the original work itself. They described the change from a history-taking style of interview, which they called the *detective inspector* approach, with the doctor conducting a search of the patient's life for significant events and feelings, to one in which the doctor listens intently to the patient's presentation, trying to tune in to how the patient wants to use the doctor and what this means. In this style of work more autonomy is left with the patient, who sets the pace, and the doctor has to be content to abandon his or her central role and follow the patient, being more aware of their relationship and less curious about secrets in the patient's inner world, or finding out what makes the patient tick. This is a more appropriate method for the brief encounters characteristic of general practice and leaves the patient's self-esteem intact. While working in this way *flash* interviews may occur, in which there is a sudden mutual awakening between doctor and patient with a consequent change in their relationship. 'Often the flash concerns the relationship between doctor and patient, but even if it does not, the relationship is changed by the flash' (Balint and Norell, 1973). Relationships in general practice often seem to progress through these 'flashes' or 'important moments' (Elder and Samuel, 1987).

Balint had a considerable literary gift and used many metaphors which are still highly resonant. He described doctors as possessing an *apostolic function* by which he meant:

> ... the way in which every doctor demonstrates a vague but almost unshakeably firm idea of how a patient ought to behave when he is ill. Although this idea is anything but explicit and concrete, it is immensely powerful, and influences the way in which the doctor not only talks to the patient and relates to him, but how he prescribes drugs, and the way in which he expects to be treated by the patient. It is almost as if every doctor had a revealed knowledge of what is right and what is wrong for patients to expect to endure, and further, as if he had a sacred duty to convert to his faith all the ignorant and unbelieving amongst his patients.   (Balint, 1957)

A doctor's apostolic function is shaped mainly by his own personality and his personal attitudes to suffering and illness but it is also influenced by the social culture in which he lives. Every culture has powerful apostolic beliefs of its own about health, as well as other things, and these are changing all the time. The apostolic attitudes of 30 years ago may no longer be relevant now. In our world, we may expect people 'to work through their grief appropriately' or 'to take responsibility for their own health, not using alcohol, coffee or tablets but learning to meditate instead'. It is worth examining what is meant by such phrases and whose concerns they reflect: the patient's or the doctor's?

Balint also often referred to the doctor as the *drug doctor*, saying he was the most frequently used drug in medical practice and calling for further study of his or her uses and side effects. Revealingly, it is the most frequently misquoted of Balint's aphorisms. Doctors usually describe the 'drug doctor' as 'the most powerful drug used in medical practice'! The apostolic function is alive and well.

General practice owes the Balints a debt of great gratitude. It is almost inconceivable to imagine people coming from positions of outside expertise, bringing the same painstaking willingness to study, listen and learn from the doctors as did the Balints, and not adopting a position of 'telling them what they ought to be doing' – an invitation that only very exceptional people can refuse.

Wider Changes

Since the 1950s, there have been many developments that have influenced general practice: vocational training has become firmly established, a Royal College of General Practitioners has been founded and departments for teaching general practice have been created in most medical schools. There has also been a rapid growth in the number of 'therapies' and 'techniques' of a broadly psychotherapeutic nature, and some of these have influenced psychotherapeutic work in general practice. Family therapy, counselling and the different approaches to sex therapy all contribute to the ways in which a general practitioner can choose to develop his or her style of work. They are like articles of clothing for the general practitioner to try on, taking some-thing from this one and other things from another one, adding to his or her range of techniques and skills alongside those acquired through his or her medical training. He or she has to find out, though, how well they fit this particular setting and how well they fit his or her particular personality. None has yet been sufficiently studied from within the particular perspective of general practice.

Body and Mind

The general practitioner has to try to achieve an integration in his or her work between those skills and attitudes that come from the more authoritarian traditions of the medical profession with those other quieter listening skills that come from the psychoanalytical tradition. When to ask questions and when to listen? He or she has to learn sufficient flexitility for the one to be part of the other.

> A young man comes to the doctor, looking rather sleepy, and complains of a heavy chest, wondering whether it could be his 'heart'. The doctor can find nothing obviously wrong. The consultation seems lifeless, but in an aside which the doctor easily might have overlooked, the patient mentions that his father died a year ago. His father had been less than 60 when he died of a heart attack and his father's father had also died young, raising the question of a familial hyperlipidaemia. The patient expresses little grief and does not feel his father's death has affected his life much. He mentions that he now visits his mother more often and seems to resent this.

The doctor has to balance her medical responsibilities, such as defining the patient's lipid status and giving him necessary advice about this, whilst also noticing her own reactions and the patient's appearance and listening for clues to this young man's heavy heart. The patient seems depressed without knowing it, quite unconsciously bringing his complaint to the doctor. He does not seem to feel as much grief as the doctor first expects. But the doctor must allow the patient's own story to unfold, without superimposing her own expectations.

This is a typical brief encounter, where there is a balance between medicine and listening, both being part of each other, not an 'either/or'. The patient has had some limited but relevant help at a time when he presented himself for it. He may leave it there or return some time later. If he does come back, the first impressions have been laid, on both the doctor's and the patient's side.

The illness or health of an individual depends on a complex interrelationship between the total person and his environment. Within the individual there is a constant interaction between the body, the mind with its powerful emotional world, both conscious and unconscious, and whatever moral and spiritual life the person has and through which he relates his life to other people and the world at large.

The doctor has a relationship with the *whole person* and often with the whole of a family too. The body and the mind reflect and influence each other all the time. There is no such easy divide as people often make. The split between the two is a very common feature of illness, where a physical tension, an ache or a rash remain quite unconnected in the patient's mind to the conflicts that may be associated with them. Medical thinking is often also split in this way with physical illness being considered first, leaving the mind as a sort of remainder. The patient is put through a sieve marked physical in order to catch only those aspects that the doctor feels he or she understands and can do something about. The antagonism sometimes observed between medical consultants and psychiatrists is an expression of this divide, with the two seeming to inhabit different worlds and psychoanalysis, in isolating the mind for particular study, is also prone to accentuating this problem.

The general practitioner is uniquely placed for an understanding and healing of this relationship. He is working across the 'body/mind' boundary practically all the time. The whole spectrum of illness is brought to him, from the almost entirely physical to the almost entirely psychological. It reflects different densities of disturbance. At the most concrete end, serious physical illnesses, such as cancers and arterial disease, always have important psychological consequences; in the middle range there are large numbers of illnesses in which body and mind seem to be inextricably bound up with each other, such as asthma, the irritable bowel syndrome, hypertension, migraine and abnormalities of menstruation; and at the lighter end there are the transient physical expressions of tension – odd pains, headaches and autonomic symptoms that come according to personal patterns of anxiety and depression.

The doctor handles, touches and listens through his stethoscope while also keeping alert and listening through his human ear as well. He examines the body at the same time as noticing the patient's reactions to this process.

Not everything has to be verbalised. If psychological tensions are expressed, which had been close to the surface anyway, their physical counterparts may resolve as well, but such connections are most often quite inaccessible. The doctor must learn to mediate his or her medicine through whatever language, be it largely physical or largely psychological, the patient is using at that time.

> Mr C. is a tall young banker in his late twenties, married to an attractive schoolteacher. They are expecting their first baby and Mrs C. comes regularly for her antenatal care. She is rather jolly and seems pleased to be pregnant. The doctor has only seen the husband once or twice before and on this occasion Mr C. seems rather more reserved than before and the two do not easily get on to the right track. He has been having intermittent diarrhoea and abdominal discomfort for some weeks. The doctor and patient fence around a bit but do not seem to get anywhere. Maybe this is the beginning of ulcerative colitis? The doctor sends him for some tests that all turn out to be normal. Mr C. is still pretty unforthcoming when he comes again, but is perhaps a little keener for the doctor to get on to the right wavelength this time and drops more of a hint. He describes his symptoms as 'blowing out' and says he is 'almost as big as his wife'.

The doctor senses an important area, makes some exploratory remarks, and when he is more sure of his footing says, 'You can look forward to the birth of babies but you can dread it too'. With doctor and patient now better tuned, the patient can express some of his feelings about the forthcoming baby: '... he hates babies, they puke and make a noise, the smaller they are the worse they are, he can't stand his friends' babies because he has seen how they have changed them, ruining their lives. ...

The patient seems to resent the intrusion of the pregnancy and is frightened by the changes that it may produce. He fears they may have to move, as there will not be enough space for the baby (or for himself?) and nowhere to retreat in peace, as he is someone who dislikes displays of strong feelings. He is angry and fears the baby will change his life, leaving him left out of the relationship between the baby and his wife. It is possible that this strong feeling of the patient's was echoed in the doctor–patient relationship where he may have felt left out by the doctor and his wife, something that very often happens in antenatal care. Perhaps they had left him with an unfair amount of the negative resentful feelings attached to the forthcoming birth? The patient afterwards felt that both sides of his experience, positive and negative (for he was also looking forward to the birth), had been accepted by the doctor, making him feel less of an outcast. He had earlier described the baby as a 'monster'. It is also possible (and there was some evidence from later joint antenatal visits) that after this consultation, Mr and Mrs C. were able to communicate with each other about such an important change in their lives in a more open and balanced way.

Still within the psychosomatic sphere, the body may literally almost break under a psychological strain.

Mr J., an earnest young man of 26, had been sent to his doctor by his employer because he had collapsed with back pain 6 weeks earlier and had still not fully recovered. The doctor had not seen him before but he gave the history of his back pain clearly. He was an only child who had always done well academically. He had 'passed everything' until recently failing some exams to become a solicitor. He had been working very hard to retake them and his parents had suggested he went away with them for a Bank Holiday weekend. He was pleased he went, but returned home earlier than his parents, in order to continue his studies. After he left, his mother had suddenly died. Normally, he would have phoned them on his safe arrival, but that night he did not. He was devastated. He had always found emotion less easy to share with his father and he adopted a role of 'carrying on', throwing himself into hard work, redoubling his efforts to do well in his retake exams. These he passed. As the pressure began to relax, only a few days later he 'collapsed' with back pain and was taken to a hospital casualty department, where he was sent home with analgesics and told to rest, advice which his firm's doctor had later repeated.

During the consultation described, in which this history emerged, the patient's emotions also emerged at the same time. He was able to break down in tears, particularly when reliving the bitter anguish he felt that his mother had not been able to share in his examination success. What had it all been for?

The patient had himself half-known that his back had cracked as a result of the tension and strain of his suppressed feelings after his mother's funeral. But he needed a doctor who could allow him to make the connection more confidently and who could help him express some of the full-hearted emotions which he had bottled up inside his body in order to carry on with his work.

'The helping him express' is often written about as 'allowing the patient to express'. It is more than that. It is the doctor experiencing some aspects of the patient's predicament and feelings, and giving them back through his or her words and reactions as a rightful experience for the patient to be having. It is a reinforced or positive echo returning to the patient from the doctor. The patient leaves feeling 'yes, that *is* what I feel'. His or her authenticity as an individual is strengthened. This is, of course, helpful only if the experience does have the feeling of *truth for the patient*. Otherwise, it may be that the feeling of conviction belongs more to the doctor's end. This is an ever-present danger.

Living in the Present

Patients often apologise when they take the doctors' time. 'I'm sorry to take up your time (again?), doctor'; 'I won't keep you a moment, doctor'. Sentences which can carry many different emphases and meanings, and which most often the doctor hardly notices. *The way* in which patients ask for the doctor's attention *matters*. Why does this patient always seem unsatisfied or unable to tolerate other patients in the waiting room? Why is this one over-apologetic and another anxiously over-friendly? *How* people present their problems to the doctor may reveal important patterns in their relationships and these may be closely related to their current difficulties. The doctor must allow such patterns to develop, being careful not to do so only to gratify his own needs, say, for patients to be appreciative or friendly. He may sense, when he is with a particular patient, that he is perceived as a parent who has to be appeased or a lover who must not come too close, an old friend or somebody the patient always has to do battle with but never completely defeat.

The doctor has to try and recognise, *there and then*, when one of these characteristic patterns of relating is being enacted with him and whether or not it is relevant. His listening must be efficient, hearing what is important at that moment.

A young woman in her thirties, Miss E., seems to the doctor prematurely grey and burdened. She has a likable seriousness about her and is depressed. She had what she describes as a big emotional breakdown 3 years ago and has been depressed on and off since. She has a strong sense of duty and seems to live in a predominantly female world. She has a responsible job which she does very conscientiously, but feels that her supervisors do not take her work seriously enough. She is new to this doctor, who can feel how heavily depressed she is, but also how difficult it is for her to do anything with this, other than to endure it worthily. He is content to let her communicate in her own way and has to remain in the dark about many of the details of various relationships she hints at as current difficulties. If he does ask or enquire, he appears to add to her burden and she says, 'Oh, it would take such a long time, it's all so complicated anyway'.

She comes seldom. On this occasion, she had not been for some time, but clearly had been very depressed. The doctor felt that he wanted her to realise that he was available for her as her doctor and finished the consultation by saying that she was able to come and see him if she felt depressed and that it was legitimate to make an appointment if she felt dreadful. It was not breaking any rules. At this point she conveyed that he had enough to deal with already and would not want to be burdened or spend more of his time seeing her. This was said genuinely, not evasively. She said it in such a way that she seemed to make *herself* responsible for *his* burden. He pointed this out to her, suggesting that she had enough to carry already, without also having to worry about his decisions in allocating his time and energy. He would look after that himself.

The doctor could feel her conflict. It was not just that she did not want to burden him. If it had been, his remarks would have made no impact. It was that she desperately wanted to burden him, but also could not allow herself to do so, and that in part her depression was related to her habit of carryng other people's responsibilities as well as her own, a pattern perhaps originally established with her parents, but certainly persisting into the present as well.

This was a crystallising point in the relationship and clearly meant something significant to her. It had arisen with the doctor, but it was important in her difficulties all round. The same or a similar point may often have come up, after all such a problem is not uncommon, but it seemed *particularly true* at that *particular moment* and was intimately related to the problems the patient was suffering in her current life. It has much of its impact for the patient because of the feelings contained in the doctor–patient encounter in which it is spoken.

Miss E. did return after quite a sort interval and this time was able to talk to the doctor more about her distress, initiating a series of appointments with him at a time when she needed help.

It is worth noting that the doctor at this stage knows nothing about the patient's father, her mother or her siblings and very little of her present relationships. He does not know about her sex life, whether she has a boyfriend, a girlfriend or no friends. If he had asked her, he would have been unable to help her in the way he did. He had to be prepared to follow the patient, trying to make sense of whatever patterns emerged.

Time

It is very often said that general practitioners do not have enough time to listen to their patients. This is far from the truth. The general practitioners' timescale is one of their setting's great strengths. They build their knowledge of their patients and the patient's families, through repeated short contacts, sometimes over many years. It is their use of the time that matters. Their appointment system is flexible. They can see a patient for 5 minutes on one occasion, 20 minutes on another. They can see people frequently for a short time and then not need to again for months. Of course, if listening is simply a process of letting people talk, then indeed they do not have enough time. But it is not. It is the accuracy of attention to the moment that counts and an ear that 'hears' what is being said in the echoes and resonances behind the patient's words. No long preamble and fact finding is needed. The doctor and patient can get to the point quickly. Much of what is important will already be known.

> Mr R., a widower in his sixties, seldom comes to the doctor, but does so one evening about 2 years after his wife's death. She had been a frequent attender whom the doctor knew well, an incessant talker with a great many complaints. Mr R. is dressed in dull clothes, near Christmas, and comes with a 'croaky cold'. No time is needed for his own doctor who has known his whole situation over the years, to understand his croaky (tearful) cold (ness) and the lack of warmth he has felt in his life since his wife's death. The doctor gives him simple treatment for his cold and a few minutes of time, tears, and some memories of the unexpectedness of her death, the shock. . . .

This is all that is necessary. A brief consultation not necessarily requiring any follow-up.

For some patients the doctor remains one of the few fixed points.

They may not come often, but know that he or she is there, as a reference point.

Most important is the patient's pattern of use over time. Is there a change? Is the patient coming more often or less often? One axis of the doctor's timescale is long term, but the rhythm of use along the way can be very variable. This reflects the distance the patient may feel he or she needs at different times, sometimes coming to the doctor for quite intense help and then staying away. This pattern itself may have important echoes.

> Miss J. is a slim 23-year-old student. She is a northerner and often comes to the surgery with a friend who stays in the waiting room. When she joined the doctor's list, she came for a repeat prescription of her pill, a routine visit in which no problems were mentioned. She returned a month later to tell the doctor she was having a difficult time with sex with her present boyfriend. She felt dry and was put off by the thought of intercourse. She was shy and embarrassed with the doctor, but told him that she had known Robert for 2 years, that he had been prepared to build up their relationship slowly which had been important for her as she had easily felt pushed into bed by men previously. She had recently changed digs and so was new to the doctor's area, but felt her present 'home' would suit her better. She had felt tense with her past family and feared that someone might walk into her bedroom at any moment if she had her boyfriend there.
>
> The doctor and Miss J. managed to establish enough contact and Miss J. would come every few weeks, sometimes more often, sometimes less, to talk to the doctor and report on progress in her relationship with Robert. The doctor had suggested seeing them together as a couple and had discussed referring them for specialist psychosexual help. Neither of these suggestions had worked out. During this time she also talked a little about her family background and other relationships. Her mother and she were 'peas in a pod'. Her father, in fact her stepfather, had been very strict but she was his 'favourite'.

The doctor felt he had to be careful not to undermine the patient's relationship with Robert, hoping instead to help Miss J. become more receptive to him.

The doctor was careful to let her dictate the pattern and frequency of her attendance, as she had clearly signalled that this was important to her in her relations with men. She did not like to be pushed. It seemed to be the doctor's task to respect this aspect of her, but not too much. He had also to push her a bit as well, towards examining some of her reactions and possible reasons for them; gently steering a course between 'too much' and 'too little'. On one occasion the doctor finished an interview feeling he had probably overdone it and gone into things more deeply than was comfortable for the patient.

However, on the next occasion she returned she look more feminine and said she had a confession to make. They had successfully made love. On that occasion her friend had not accompanied her to the waiting room.

This kind of work tends to progress, then run into new difficulties – backwards and forwards. Miss J. seemed to keep attending when she wanted to and the doctor continued to try and balance his encouragement with allowing her to set the pace.

This work goes on amidst all the other demands that are made on a doctor's attention. She has many other difficult tasks to perform and her mind may often be far from being tuned into her patients. The doctor will need to find a balance for herself between engaging and identifying with her patients, on the one hand, and gaining sufficient distance from them, on the other, for thoughtful professional reflection. She will need both if she is to remain useful to her patients and neither become too defensive and distant or 'clinical', nor be too close to think clearly and see her patients from an angle different from the one at which they see themselves. She can then show respect for her patient's own way of living and treat the patient as another human being and not only as the bearer of a diagnosis for the doctor to discover.

I have isolated some aspects of the general practitioner's work in order to draw attention to the possibilities the setting offers for psychotherapeutic work of a certain kind. I hope that some of the characteristics of this work can be seen from the cases I have discussed, all taken from a general practitioner's everyday work: the doctor's relatively easy personal accessibility; his involvement with patients at times of need and change; his 'being there' for people (regardless of how often consulted) for long periods of time, often for many years; his relationship with the *whole* patient; the fact that the patient holds the key and can therefore dictate the pace, coming at a time of his own making (*Why now?* What is important to *this* patient at *this* time?); listening all round the patient as well as to echoes in himself; being content to do *just enough* and not more, so that the patient may leave feeling free to use the doctor at another time, or in a different way, without having to bear his soul more than he wants or having his life interpreted to him. The patient remains in charge of his own life and, hopefully, is strengthened and not undermined by his contact with the doctor.

References

BALINT, M. (1954). Training general practitioners in psychotherapy. *British Medical Journal* 1, 115.

BALINT, M. (1955). The doctor, his patient and the illness. *The Lancet* i, 683.

BALINT, M. (1957). *The Doctor, His Patient and the Illness*. London: Pitman Medical.

BALINT, M., HUNT, J., JOYCE, D. et al. (1970). *Treatment or Diagnosis: A Study of Repeat Prescriptions in General Practice*. London: Tavistock Publications.

BALINT, E. and NORELL, J.S. (eds) (1973). *Six Minutes for the Patient*. London: Tavistock Publications.

BROWN, D. and PEDDER, J. (1979). *Introduction to Psychotherapy*. London: Tavistock Publications.

COLLINGS, J.S. (1950). General practice in England today: A renaissance. *Lancet* i, 555.

COURTENAY, M.J.F. (1968). *Sexual Discord in Marriage*. London: Tavistock Publications.

ELDER, A. and SAMUEL, O. (eds) (1987). *'While I'm here, doctor.'* London: Tavistock Publications.

GOLDBERG, D.P. and BLACKWELL, B. (1970). Psychiatric illness in general practice. *British Medical Journal* 1, 439.

HOPKINS, P. (1956). Referrals in general practice. *British Medical Journal* 2, 873.

MILLER, P.McC., INGHAM, J.B.and DAVIDSON, S. (1976). Life events symptoms and social support. *Journal of Psychosomatic Research* 20, 515.

ROYAL COLLEGE OF GENERAL PRACTITIONERS (1981). Prevention of Psychiatric Disorders in General Practice. *Report of General Practice 20*. London: RCGP.

TUNNADINE, D. and GREEN, R. (1978). *Unwanted Prengancy – Accident or Illness?* Oxford: Oxford University Press.

WINNICOTT, D.W. (1972) *The Maturational Process and the Facilitating Environment*. (The International Psychoanalytical Library, No. 64.) London: Hogarth Press.

Chapter 7
Group Psychotherapy

DICK BLACKWELL

Introduction

This chapter has six sections. The first provides an historical background, placing group psychotherapy in the context of the twin developments of sociological and psychological theories. Next is described the structure and process of psychotherapy groups, covering aspects of membership, duration, types of groups and how they function. The third section refers to the training of group psychotherapists, followed by a discussion as to how the group psychotherapy process is thought to work. The fifth section addresses the question of which patients to refer, while finally a look is taken at wider applications of group psychotherapy outside the purely clinical setting.

Historical Background

The study of human beings and their relationship with their world has a long history, going back at least as far as the Ancient Greek philosophers over 2000 years ago. However, it was only in the nineteenth century that the discipline of sociology began to take shape and to formulate methods of studying whole societies scientifically. Durkheim, in his classic study of suicide, was one of the first to describe how individual behaviour can be understood as a function of social phenomena. Suicide, which had previously been understood as a most individual act, could now be seen as significantly influenced by social factors, i.e. by a person's relationship with others. Marx, too, argued that a person's whole being was essentially a function of his or her social relationships. Although the precise ways in which social relationships influence individuals continue to be matters of further exploration and debate, the fundamental premise that human social relationships are a crucial dimension of human well-being now seems firmly established.

The first third of the twentieth century saw the development, within sociology, of a concern not only with whole societies and classes that had been the focus of the nineteenth century pioneers, but also with interactions between small numbers of individuals. Sociologists such as Meade and Cooley began to study small social units and the way these influenced the individual's experience of him- or herself. It was at this time that groups began to be used therapeutically.

Joseph Pratt began a group for tuberculosis patients in Boston in 1905, Edward Lazell in Washington treated schizophrenics in 1919, Trigant Burrow treated neurotics in 1920, Alfred Adler used groups generally in 1921, Julius Metzel worked with alcoholics, Cody Marsh used lecture and group discussion in New York in 1930, J.L. Moreno began psychodrama in the 1930s, and Sam Slavson worked with disturbed children and subsequently established the idea of the small group whose structure and process provide the basis of much modern group psychotherapy. It is not clear how directly these pioneers were influenced by the sociological studies, but it is clear that both sociologists and group therapists were participating in the same trend towards an increased understanding of individuals in the context of their relationship with others.

This first third of the century also saw the development of psychoanalysis by Sigmund Freud and his colleagues. Freud was initially a clinician concerned with the treatment of individual patients but he rapidly became a major thinker about the nature and development of the human psyche in relation to its environment. Although he sought to apply his theories to the behaviour of small and large groups, and to whole societies, the individual remained the principle focus of his investigations through his psychoanalytical work. His theories of society were therefore based on his theories of the individual, whereas the sociologists proceeded in the opposite direction, to theories of the individual based on the study of groups and societies.

The last 50 years have seen an increasing integration of these two orientations, particularly in the theory and practice of work with small groups of between six and twelve people. This work shows four distinct strands of development: that of Kurt Lewin (1952) with training groups (T groups); the work of Wilfred Bion (1961) analysing the group as a single psychic unit; the investigations of Wolf and Schwartz (1965) doing psychoanalysis of individuals within the group setting; and particularly S.H. Foulkes (1948) who utilised the communication between group members as a therapeutic transaction.

Lewin emigrated from Germany during the rise of Nazism in the 1930s and settled in the USA. He conducted research on the effect of group membership on individuals and developed the theory of the social field in which each individual existed. This was derived from the concept of a force field in physics. His work was applied in organizations and used widely in management training programmes.

Bion was an English psychoanalyst working as an army psychiatrist when he began his work on groups. Based at the Northfield Military Hospital outside Birmingham, he addressed problems of group morale and was a key instigator of what became one of the first 'therapeutic communities'. He studied the group as a single unit and tried to develop group specific concepts. But ultimately he further explained these group concepts in terms of the psychoanalytical theories of Freud and Melanie Klein (the latter had significantly advanced psychoanalytical theory by applying it to the study and treatment of children). Bion thus produced a psychoanalytical theory of groups which has had considerable influence on the development of group psychotherapy in the UK. It has also been used, as has Lewin's theory, in the understanding of organisations and in management training and consultancy.

Wolk and Schwartz were American psychoanalysts who developed a form of group therapy focused on the individual. The group setting enabled them to observe the way each individual behaved in relation to the others. They could then comment on this individual behaviour and offer insights to each one in the traditional psychoanalytical way. They did not apply any particular theories of group behaviour. They regarded the group as a setting in which individual proclivities were revealed and exposed for analysis, rather than seeing group process in itself as an agent of change.

Foulkes was, like Lewin, an émigré from Nazi Germany, coming to England during the 1930s. In Germany he had been closely associated with the Frankfurt Institute for Social Research and his thinking was significantly influenced by the sociological work undertaken there. Like Bion, he worked at the Northfield Military Hospital and played a major part in the development of the 'therapeutic community' there. He was also a psychoanalyst who applied psychoanalytical concepts to the understanding of groups. But he saw the process of interaction *between* members of the group as the primary therapeutic process. The role of the group therapist was to facilitate, or in his word 'conduct', this process. His term 'conductor' to describe the group therapist's role was analogous to the conductor of an orchestra, in which the members of the orchestra make the music, in combination with each other, with the conductor enabling this process and interpreting the musical themes. He regarded the individual as an inherently social being and regarded symptoms as disorders of social interaction, inarticulate ways of communicating with others. His theories, along with those of Bion, constitute the major strands of group psychotherapy in the UK.

In addition to these four strands, five other developments are worthy of note. The first is the development of psychodrama by Moreno in the USA. This was concerned with creating dramatic scenarios, such as role plays and simulations which enabled individuals to experience and express emotions that had often been suppressed or of which they were not normally aware. Psychodrama is now a growing therapeutic mode in this country and is sometimes combined with other approaches as well as being used in its own right. It was Moreno who introduced the term 'group therapy' in 1925.

Secondly, there has been the work of Gregory Bateson (1972) and his associates studying communication between people. Combining theories of psychoanalysis, anthropology, epistemology and biology, their work provided the theoretical underpinnings for the rapid growth of family therapy over the last 25 years. They, as Foulkes, saw symptoms as aspects or functions of interactional processes between people, specifically people in the intimate relationships of family life. Whereas Foulkes applied this orientation to work with 'stranger groups' – i.e. groups of people who were not otherwise known to each other – family therapists developed techniques for working directly with those social networks in which symptoms were occurring.

Thirdly, there has been the growth of the encounter group movement, often associated with the West Coast of the USA, but widely known and employed throughout the Western World. Carl Rogers (1970) and Fritz Perls (1971) were both pioneers in this field. Lewin's T groups contributed to some of the developments in this area, which also includes the psychologist Abraham Maslow (1968) and the school of gestalt psychology among its influences. Encounter groups are concerned with promoting the honest and open expression of feelings between people, that is seen as an inherently healthy and growth enhancing process. Such groups have tended to receive a 'bad press' in more conventional psychotherapeutic quarters, but more detailed study reveals significant similarities between some types of encounter group and more conventional psychotherapy groups (Lieberman et al., 1973).

Fourthly, there is the therapeutic community movement. Tom Main (1946), first at Northfield Military Hospital and subsequently at the Cassel Hospital in Surrey, and Maxwell Jones at the Henderson Hospital, also in Surrey, have been the major pioneers of this approach within the National Health Service. Other important contributions outside the NHS have come from Elly Jansen (1980) at the Richmond Fellowship, R.D. Laing at Kingsley Hall in East London and Joe Berke and Morton Schatzman at the Arbours Association in North London. Therapeutic communities mobilise the curative powers of the group on a 24-hours-a-day basis. The patients, usually called members, residents or even guests, live together in hospital, hostel or other type of dwelling forming their own community. Each member plays an active part in the running of the community's affairs. The staff participate too and help to enable the ingredients of communal life, such as cooperating, competing, supporting, challenging, to become therapeutic processes.

Finally, one of the most recent developments, which is currently being pioneered by Pat de Maré (1985), is the study of a large group. He has employed the large group, numbering from 15 to 40 members, in the treatment of individual patients. But he is also concerned with its development as a social phenomenon, believing that the capacity for people to engage in dialogue in such an arena not only has a civilising effect on the individual (i.e. developing qualities of citizenship in a participatory democracy), but can also have a humanising effect on society.

The foregoing overview will have given some idea of the breadth of the field of group psychotherapy. As a group analyst, much of what the author has to say will inevitably reflect that orientation and may not necessarily hold true for other styles of group therapy. However, much of it will be generally applicable to what the author would call conventional group psychotherapy, i.e. group psychotherapy as practised generally within the NHS and in other settings, by practitioners with psychoanalytical or psychodynamic orientations and an awareness of the importance of social process.

Structure and Process of Psychotherapy Groups

Frequency and duration

Groups usually meet once weekly, although twice weekly or fortnightly meetings are possible variations. They usually meet for one and a half hours and great importance is attached to prompt starts and finishes, although a therapist may occasionally allow a few extra minutes if he or she deems it necessary to achieve an appropriate ending to the session.

Membership

The group will usually have between five and nine members, selected by the therapist to achieve a suitable mixture for the purposes of the group. In some groups all the patients will have been brought together because they have the same problem, for example alcoholism, drug addiction, sexual dysfunction, school refusal etc. Alternatively, they may have an assortment of different problems. Likewise, with regard to age and gender, a group may be all of one sex or mixed; it may contain a very narrow age band, e.g. sufferers from mid-life crises, or have a wide spread from 20 to 65. It is preferable, however, to aim for balance in that no one feels him- or herself to be 'out on a limb'. If the group contains both sexes, it is best to have as near as possible an equal number of each sex. If there is not to be just one problem represented, then there should be a good assortment. Five alcoholics, a depressive and someone with sexual difficulties would be unlikely to provide a useful mix. Also it is not a good idea to have one member much older or much younger than the rest. In short, the group should either be fully homogeneous along any particular dimension, or fully heterogeneous.

Opinions vary regarding the relative merits of hetero- vs homogeneous groupings. It is argued, on the one hand, that patients get early comfort and support from others with whom they have much in common. This, along with the reassurance that they are not alone in their predicament, can speed the early phases of the group's development and may also lead to more enduring understanding and intimacy which will promote the therapeutic process. On the other hand, such a group may lack the variety, difference in perspective and therefore, new information that is available in heterogeneous groups. Homogeneous groups may share common blind spots and will have only the therapist to challenge them.

Co-therapy

There is usually just one therapist to each group except where there are specific reasons for having two people working as co-therapists. Couples' groups, where marital or co-habiting partners come together with other couples, is an example in which co-therapy is widely used. Co-therapy may also be helpful for inexperienced therapists, either learning by partnering a more experienced colleague or working with another inexperienced colleague for mutual support and confidence. Co-therapy can also provide valuable learning for experienced therapists who may be put 'on their mettle' by the presence of a potentially critical colleague. At the same time, they may find the presence of a colleague provides them with the security to be more adventurous as therapists. It is also likely that groups which have no special reason for requiring it can nevertheless benefit considerably from the input of two therapists instead of one. On the other hand, co-therapists need to be able to play together like tennis partners and, if they cannot harmonise their input and resolve their own inevitable differences, they will considerably handicap the group.

Closed and open groups

Closed groups run for a fixed period of time with the same members. They may meet for as few as six or twelve sessions, or they may continue for a year or more. New members do not join during the course of the group, even if one or more of the original members drop out.

Open groups do take in new members as others leave and usually have no fixed time period. They may continue for many years, during which time they will completely renew their membership. Patients remain in these groups for varied periods. From 18 months to 2 years is usually regarded as a minimum period for full benefit to be derived from the group. However, some patients may stay for over 5 years, not necessarily in order to resolve their initial difficulty but often because they continue to derive other benefits from being in the group.

Group process

When they meet, the group members sit in a circle with the therapist or therapists.* They will usually stay in their seats for the whole meeting since the process is essentially one of verbal and visual communication. The therapist will not generally ask them to change places, move about or touch each other, nor will he or she expect them to do so spontaneously. Inevitably, however, there will be times when one member will extend a comforting hand to another in distress and the therapist is unlikely to regard this as against the rules. There are a few conventional group psychotherapists who will, from time to time, incorporate psychodrama techniques into group therapy and would then have their patients moving about accordingly.

There is no formal agenda for group discussion and the therapist will not initially offer any direction. He or she will leave the group to talk about anything they want to bring up and to get to know each other in whatever way they choose. The therapist will allow this process to develop, watching and listening, and will then contribute in his or her own way to enable the group members to learn from their own experience of the process in which they are participating. The sort of interventions the therapist makes will depend on the personal style and the theoretical orientation of that particular therapist.

Among the possible contributions of the therapist are the following: questioning of either the whole group or individuals to elicit information or to encourage further thought and exploration of a particular issue, e.g. 'How old were you when your father died?'; 'How do you feel about what M has just said?'; disagreeing with a particular statement made or a position taken by a group member, e.g. 'I disagree with your view that sex should not be discussed in the group'; drawing attention to aspects of group or individual behaviour which have not been noticed by the participants, e.g. 'I notice that every time A and B get angry with each other, J clutches the arms of his chair very tightly' and 'Every time P brings up his jealousy, someone else quickly changes the subject'; interpretation of unconscious themes, e.g. 'You have talked a lot about competition in your jobs, I think you are also referring to the competition here in the group'. Sometimes the group will lapse into silence. At such times, the therapist will usually wait with the group until the conversation is resumed. He will only break the silence if he feels he has something particular to say at that point. He will not see it as his responsibility to keep the conversation going.

---

* The rest of this explanation will assume only one therapist.

Training of Group Psychotherapists

It is generally agreed that group therapists need to have their own experience of receiving therapy. They must know themselves and how they respond to others, and how others respond to them. Some schools of thought would regard individual therapy as an adequate preparation for a trainee therapist, whilst others would insist on experience as a patient in a group. The Institute of Group Analysis requires its trainees to spend at least 3 years as patients in an analytical group.

In addition to having therapy themselves, trainees will study one or more of the theories of group process and of problem or symptom formation and resolution. They will usually spend 2 years conducting one or more groups under supervision. This supervision may involve meeting individually with a supervisor to report on and discuss the group but, more usually, it will involve meeting with other trainees in a group led by the supervisor. The supervisory process will then reflect certain important dimensions of the therapeutic process.

How does Group Psychotherapy work?

There are a number of theories about how group psychotherapy works. These cover different views about how symptoms and problems arise and how they are resolved.

In the traditional psychoanalytical view, symptoms are manifestations of internal conflicts in the unconscious part of the individual's mind. These conflicts date back to infancy when ideas, wishes, desires and accompanying fears were 'repressed' from consciousness. This repression results from social prohibitions such as the incest taboo or from fantasies such as the male child's fear of being castrated for having incestuous desires. In psychoanalytical psychotherapy the patient re-enacts the infant–parent relationship in the patient–therapist relationship. The patient is said to 'regress' to the infantile state and to transfer on to the therapist the feelings that the infant had for his or her parents. In this way the repressed ideas, wishes, desires and fears begin to manifest themselves. The therapist draws the patient's attention to them so that they can become conscious, be expressed verbally and 'worked through'.

In a psychotherapy group, these unconscious features of the infant–parent relationship become transferred on to other group members as well as to the therapist and even the group itself may be experienced as if it were a parent, usually the mother. Group members may also represent siblings for each other.

Other theories lay more emphasis on present conflicts and difficulties, and de Maré (1985) has introduced the term 'transposition' to describe the way in which a patient treats other group members not as figures from the past (infancy) but as figures from the present – spouses, lovers, friends, colleagues, enemies, rivals etc. In this view, whole constellations of relationships can be transposed and re-enacted within the group. In this way, patients can become more aware of how they deal with problems in relationships with others and can experiment in the group setting with different ways of relating.

This view sees problems and symptoms arising in an individual's relationships with others. The headache which repels unwelcome sexual advances is an example that has entered contemporary folklore. In a group setting, sufferers from these headaches may learn to say 'no' more directly when not wising to comply with another's wishes. Or in those cases where no does not just mean no, but is also an expression of feelings of anger, sadness, resentment or fear, a patient may also learn to recognise these feelings and express them more directly.

Irving Yalom (1970) has developed the following list of 'curative factors' which operate in groups: installation of hope, universality (the discovery of being like everyone else), imparting of information, altruism, corrective recapitulation of the primary group, development of socialising techniques, imitative behaviour, interpersonal learning, group cohesiveness and catharsis. He regards these as all interlinked in the dynamic process of the group.

Skynner (1983) has attempted to connect historical factors of infantile relationships in the family of origin with contemporary relationship difficulties. He suggests that the individual grows up in a family in which certain aspects of emotional life are avoided. These may be anger, jealousy, rivalry, intimacy, sadness, sexuality etc. The individual's repertoire of behaviour and communication is consequently limited by growing up in this context. Furthermore, he evolves a philosophy of life, chooses friends and enemies, jobs and pastimes, lovers and spouses in accordance with this limited repertoire. In turn, as a parent, he will influence the development of his children in a similar way. If at any point the individual encounters a situation for which his existing repertoire has no satisfactory response, he will encounter an apparently insoluble problem or develop a symptom that brings him to therapy. Because of the diversity and variety of interaction in a therapy group, the patient is likely to encounter the very situation that was avoided in his family and which the patient has successfully avoided prior to the occurrence of the problem or symptom presented for therapy. In the group, the patient has to deal with the situation and experience the avoided emotion. It is only after he has done this that he is able to have insight and look back on his previous patterns of avoidance. This theory is particularly interesting in that it describes a scenario of change which need not necessarily be confined to the therapy situation. Such challenges to a person's habitual ways of relating, which were learned in the family of origin, can occur in other areas of life where they cannot be avoided. Thus, psychotherapy is not the only arena in which change and growth takes place. This is in contrast to more traditional psychoanalytical theories which suggest that such change and growth can be achieved only through regression and interpretation of infantile conflicts in the psychotherapeutic setting.

Foulkes (1948) regarded symptoms as forms of communication. They were the result of disorders in the social network of the individual patient who became the locus for the expression of the disorder. Foulkes regarded the group process as essentially one of communication in which symptoms can be seen to be 'inarticulate' ways of communicating. Through the therapy group process, the individual can learn to communicate more satisfactorily. He will then be able to improve the patterns of communication within his social network, which were the source of the original symptom. Foulkes developed the concept of the group matrix to describe the complex 'trans-personal' network of communication which emerges in a group. As was noted in the historical background, his view has marked similarities to that of Bateson (1972) and the family therapy tradition. Bateson also regarded symptoms as arising from communication patterns in social networks, particularly families, so that changed communication would be the thera-peutic goal. He focused on 'levels' of communication and learning and applied the theory of logical types developed by the philosophers Russell and Whitehead. This resulted in the famous double-bind theory of schizo-phrenia. But perhaps because this focus was so specifically on families, his theories are widely applied in family therapy but not as yet in group therapy.

Who to refer for Group Psychotherapy

Again, there is diversity of opinion on this subject. Some therapists have very clear ideas on which diagnostic categories can be helped by group therapy and which cannot. However, Rutan and Stone (1984) point out that 'most exclusionary recommendations in the literature can be countered by other published recommendations that such patients are treatable in groups'. There is also disagreement as to whether traditional psychiatric or even psycho-analytical diagnostic categories are actually useful in deciding on a patient's suitability for a group. It is my view that these categories are not very useful, because the success of therapy depends much more on how a particular patient 'gets on' with a particular therapist. Such matching is quite idiosyncratic.

The classification of patients in whatever diagnostic terms can provide only crude guidelines. What is really valuable is for medical practitioners to make personal contact with the psychotherapists to whom they might refer patients for psychotherapy. Obviously, there are limitations to this but, as a general guideline, the better a referrer knows the therapist, the more able he or she will be to make appropriate referrals. A discussion between practitioner and therapist about the *possibility* of referring a particular patient for therapy is in the author's view invaluable to all concerned, and such preliminary pre-referrral discussions will also offer doctor and therapist an opportunity to make contact.

Medical students with whom the author has discussed this seem to feel it is incumbent on them to decide whether or not a patient should be referred for therapy. As doctors already have to carry a great deal of responsibility, there seems no good reason for expecting them to carry this additional and unnecessary burden which should more appropriately be shared with their psychotherapist colleagues.

The therapist assessing a patient for a group is concerned not only with how he or she gets on with the patient, but also with how the patient will relate to other members of the group. Apart from being concerned with having a balanced group in terms of age, sex and other dimensions described in the section on group composition, the therapist will also have an intuitive sense of how certain patients might relate to each other. However, despite this need for each group therapist to consider each referral on its own merits, it is possible to make some tentative generalisations to aid referrers, both in terms of who might benefit and who might not.

Clearly, the major criterion must be the view that a particular symptom is amenable to psychological treatment. Many illnesses previously regarded as purely physical are now thought to have a significant psychological component. Medical practitioners themselves will differ in the extent to which they regard such ailments as tuberculosis, cancer, asthma, premenstrual tension, allergies etc. as suitable for psychological as well as physical treatment. It is also important that the patient him- or herself is prepared to seek psychological help. A patient convinced, despite his doctor's opinion, that there is no psychological component in his complaint is likely to enter a therapy group with the intention of failing to improve in order to demonstrate the irrelevance of group therapy to his particular problem. Such an attitude suggests a poor prognosis.

This willingness of the patient to try to use group therapy positively applies equally, if more obviously, with psychological symptoms. Whilst the value of group therapy may be obvious to the doctor and psychotherapist, it may not necessarily be obvious to the patient. It is important to distinguish between the patient who is anxious and uncertain about trying something new, but will respond to encouragement and explanation, and the patient who is just not willing to make the investment of time and energy necessary to benefit from group therapy. The former may have a good chance of benefiting from it; the latter is virtually assured of failure.

As well as the type of unmotivated patient described above, there are some other contraindications. One of these is a lack of impulse control, such that the safety of other group members is at risk. Another is an immediate crisis requiring immediate help, with no time to enter a group and establish relationships that can lead to change. Having a speech impediment or other difficulties with language sufficient to inhibit ordinary conversation are also contraindications. In short, if a patient is able and willing to join a group and to participate in its process as outlined above, he or she has the possibility of benefiting from it. Anything that prevents this process from taking place can be deemed a contraindication.

Wider Application of Group Psychotherapy

As indicated in the description of the historical development of group psychotherapy, its theories and techniques have not been confined to the field of psychiatry. Group therapy approaches are now commonly used, albeit in modified forms, in education, industry and with staff groups in both health and social services. Usually, the aim of such applications is to facilitate more open and effective communication between groups of people working together. It also provides an opportunity for discussion and sharing of the stresses and strains affecting both individuals and groups in their work setting. In education, Abercrombie has pioneered the use of group approaches to teaching university students (Abercrombie and Terry, 1978). She adopted a group psychotherapeutic approach to create a non-authoritarian climate in seminars which enabled students to learn actively through discussion with each other, rather than passively by being given informaton and knowledge of the tutor.

Skynner worked with the staff of a comprehensive school. They met as a group to discuss the difficulties they had with the pupils. This resulted in a substantial decrease in the number of referrals from the school to the local child guidance clinic.

Groups are also used for training staff. The emphasis here is not on the functioning of a work group but on the individual development of the members. These groups may be used on management training courses where the participants do not share the same work setting. It is thought that the understanding of themselves and others that participants gain from the group experience will enable them to function more effectively in their jobs.

These developments are not yet as extensive as they might be. They are still only the beginnings of the extending of knowledge gained in psychotherapy to other areas of life, and extending the knowledge gained in those other areas back into psychotherapy. They are also beginnings in understanding the common dimensions of therapy, education, personal development and social change.

References

ABERCROMBIE, M.L.J. and TERRY, P. M. (1978). *Talking to Learn: Improving Teaching and Learning in Small Groups*. Society for Research in Higher Education, University of Surrey, Guildford.

BATESON, G. (1972). *Steps to an Ecology of Mind*. New York: Ballantine.

BION, W.R. (1961). *Experience in Groups*. London: Tavistock Publications.

DE BOARD, R. (1978). *The Psychoanalysis of Organisations*. London: Tavistock Publications.

DE MARÉ, P.B. (1985). Large group perspectives. *Group Analysis* 18, 2.

FOULKES, S.H. (1948). *Introduction to Group Analytic Psychotherapy*. London: Heinemann.

JANSEN, E. (1980). *The Therapeutic Community*. London: Croom Helm.

JONES, M. (1953). *The Therapeutic Community*. New York: Basic Books.

LEWIN, K. (1952). Defining the field at a given time. In D. Cartwright (Ed.), *Field Theory in Social Sciences*. New York: Basic Books.

LIEBERMAN, M.A., YALOM, I.D. and MILES, M.B. (1973). *Encounter Groups: First Facts*. New York: Basic Books.

MAIN, T.F. (1946). The hospital as a therapeutic institution. *Bulletin of the Menninger Clinic* 10, 66.

MASLOW, A. (1968). *Toward a Psychology of Being*. New York: D. Van Nostrand.

PERLS, F.S. (1971). *Gestalt Therapy Verbatim*. New York: Bantam.

ROGERS, C. (1970). *Carl Rogers on Encounter Groups*. New York: Harper & Row.

RUTAN, J.S. and STONE, W.N. (1984). *Psychodynamic Group Psychotherapy*. Lexington: Collamore Press.

SKYNNER, A.C.R. (1983). Group analysis and family therapy. *International Journal of Group Psychotherapy*. 34.

WOLF, A. and SCHWARTZ, E.K. (1965). *Psychoanalysis in Groups*. New York: Grune & Stratton.

YALOM, I.D. (1970). *The Theory and Practice of Group Psychotherapy*. New York: Basic Books.

Chapter 8
Therapy, the Family and Others

ALAN COOKLIN

Individual psychotherapies, whether based on a model of learning theory or on psychodynamic understanding, have one thing in common. They view the patient from the standpoint that he or she is an integrated discreet organism. Family and other 'systems' therapies view the patient as one component in a system or 'organism' (e.g. the family) which many manifest its malfunction through the behaviour of that component – the patient. That is the major difference.

The purpose of this chapter is to elaborate that difference, the thinking behind it, some of the evidence which supports that thinking and implications for intervention. The goal is that the practitioner should be stimulated to think of alternative ways to use his or her professional skill, in order to promote healthy changes in families and other human systems. It is not a chapter on 'How to be a family therapist' nor on 'What family therapists do'. Its aim is to offer the practitioner a broader view of the context of human psychological distress and thus to broaden the range of therapeutic options in the practitioner's repertoire.

To this end, the chapter will be organised in 15 sections:

1. What is family therapy, both as a treatment and as a framework of conceptualisation?
2. The family interactional model of psychiatry in relation to other models.
3. Theories of organisation and interaction in families.
4. Family patterns and the 'family dance'.
5. Short-term patterns and patterns over time.
6. Balance and stability vs change in the family.
7. The question of intervention: Does it work? Is it worth it? What are the dangers?
8. Some aspects of family therapy – how it operates.
9. Clinical example.
10. Various methods of therapy with the family.

11. Family therapy: comparison of principles with individual psycho-
    therapy and group psychotherapy.
12. Impacts of race, ethnicity and social disadvantages.
13. Applications to different kinds of family structure and to 'non-family'
    human systems.
14. What can the practitioner do?
15. Further reading and opportunities for learning and training.

What is Family Therapy?

Family therapy refers, on the one hand, to a 'treatment' – an activity whereby
a therapist sits down for one or more sessions with various members of a
family to help them change something – and, on the other hand, to a
framework for conceptualisation, a way of understanding and thinking
about human behaviour which may then be used in a variety of ways. This
thinking can then be applied to the family or to other contexts in which
human beings live in proximity and may develop intimate relationships.

Two important components of the thinking are first that people are not
islands, and their behaviour can only be understood in the context in which it
occurs. Using this thinking, the idea of a person having an 'internal' world is
different from using a framework in which the individual is considered in
isolation. The internal world is no longer a 'closed shop', viewed only
through the portal of dreams and other channels of the unconscious, but is
accessible through the day-to-day interactions with others. These interactions themselves are then dependent on the context in which they occur.
Consider the behaviour of a young mother towards an infant. If the
'individual' perspective is taken to absurd extremes, the mother's behaviour
could be seen principally in terms of her unconscious fantasies about the
child, or her learned responses. Alternatively, it could be recognised that the
mother's behaviour will be affected by many factors. In some Indian cultures
she would expect the child to be in almost constant physical contact with her
for the first year or so of life, whilst in many Western milieux she might
expect to have longish periods of separation from the child very soon after
birth. Her responsiveness, and its degree of flexibility or rigidity, the degree
of playfulness, anxiety, attentiveness or 'over-attentiveness' will also be
affected by the child's response to her. If she perceives herself as looking after
the child in a relatively hostile environment, she may be highly protective of
every aspect of her child's life. This pattern is likely to be intensified in
situations of racial conflict or prejudice. In the first few weeks or months of
life, this will give the child the freedom to develop. However, the context
changes with time. The same behaviour on the mother's part when the child
reaches 2, 3, 4 or 5 years of age may have the effect of no longer being
protective but of becoming restrictive. On the other hand, if the child is

developing in a context in which there are real dangers – such as from racial attack – then this behaviour may continue to be appropriately protective for a much longer period. The mother's and, therefore, the child's behaviour will also be heavily influenced by their relationships with others in their environment. For example, if the mother feels well supported by her husband, she will be less likely to perceive the environment as hostile and therefore be less liable to protect the child inappropriately. However, if her parents are seen as in competition with her husband, or if his family is seen as in competition with hers, the mother may be encouraged to isolate herself further with her child as a mutual protection. These factors will have a major impact on an only child whilst, if there are many siblings, the effect will be diluted.

A second component of this thinking is that people in close physical and emotional proximity readily set up stable patterns of interaction. These patterns are made up from a whole series of sequences; repetitive short events involving two or more people. This will be elaborated on later under 'Family patterns and the family dance'. If the family presents a problem, either as an individual's symptom or behaviour, or as a set of 'problem' relationships, it is assumed that this problem is a manifestation of the total organisation of the family. It is not so much that the family 'causes' the problem, but rather that the problem, as it develops, is part of the life and context of the family and can soon become part of what is familiar and comforting. A practitioner who does 'family therapy' will, therefore, be concerned with the total family organisation and how this relates to the problem, rather than to any one individual. To do this he or she may use various methods, may work through individuals, but keeping his or her sights on the whole organism of the family. He or she may work with parts of the family, with the whole nuclear family or with the nuclear and extended family of three generations or more, or even include other members of the community (especially where the family is an ethnic minority in the host culture). The therapy may last for one, two or many sessions of one or more hours. The most common is for the therapist to work for a fairly small number of sessions, averaging about ten.

The Family Interactional Mode of Psychiatry in Relation to Other Models

Although psychiatry is a branch of medicine, to operate rationally it has to link all levels of human experience: physical, cognitive, perceptual, emotional and, in certain circumstances, philosophical and theological. It is therefore not surprising that, in the struggle to achieve some coherence, there has been much controversy about the correct focus for the subject. The proponents of these different views inevitably communicate a different kind of relationship with the patients who seek, or are brought for, their help (Cooklin, 1973). The family interactional model implies not only a different relationship to include others, but might be expressed as: 'You present me with distress or disturbance. I see this disturbance as representing a problem in the organisation of which you are a part, the family. Therefore, I will not respond directly to you: rather, I shall attempt to examine and change the organisation of the family in the belief that this will also be of most benefit to you.'

The family interactional model is, therefore, concerned with the patient as part of a group, rather than just the relationship between patient and practitioner. It also differs in the way in which it approaches causality: the family interactional model does not imply that the family is noxious and has 'made the patient ill'. Rather, it is concerned with the way in which a number of factors, particularly the family organisation and the interactional pattern in the family, have allowed part of the patient's behaviour to be congruent to the family's way of living, whilst another part of the behaviour remains incongruent. Consider a young anorectic girl in a family where the members have been used to being close and physically intimate with each other, in which conflicts have usually been kept at a low ebb and in which unity of the family has been highly valued. The girl's behaviour is discordant to the family in that she arouses much anxiety and, in such a family, feeding may have been highly valued. On the other hand, it may be congruent to the family in that her sexual development is delayed, she will take less interest in and be less attractive to boys, thus avoiding conflicts common in most families. She will stay at home closely involved with her family, and her behaviour will keep other members of the family closely involved with her. One approach to the problem would be to consider the implications of the family adapting to a growing adolescent girl, to consider how the conflicts which would arise could be handled differently by her and the family. Such an approach would be addressing principally the organisation of the family.

Theories of Organisation and Interaction in Families

Two related sets of ideas have provided frameworks for considering the family as a system rather than just a set of individuals. These are general systems theory and cybernetics (Ashby, 1956; Bertalanffy, 1968).

General systems theory

General systems theory is not a theory of causality, but a theory of organisation. It is a way of categorising systems throughout nature both living and inanimate. It considers the family as a living system and considers its capacity to adapt in terms of the following.

The boundary around the family and around the subsystems in the family

This relates to the degree to which family members maintain a close unity within the family, or engage actively with the outside world. This, in turn, controls the input and output of information to and from the family. Information includes people. Thus a family with a very impermeable boundary will be likely to adapt poorly to the arrival of new members – babies, grandparents, boy- or girlfriends – and will be intolerant of members moving out (such as around the time of adolescence).

The theory also considers the differentiation of the subsystems within the family and the degree to which the boundary around these is clear

For example, the marital relationship is a separate subsystem from, say, the parental subsystem. In a family in which the members say 'we always do everything together', the differentiation of the parents having a separate relationship may be poorly recognised. This, in turn, may militate against the development of any other set of separate relationships.

Suprasystems and subsystems

In addition to the degree to which the family is differentiated into sub-systems, it will also form part of other suprasystems to varying degrees. For example, the family may be part of an extended family network and the different members may be part of other suprasystems within the community – work, school, social groups etc.

Cybernetics

Cybernetics is a set of principles adapted from electronic control systems. The thermostat in a central heating system is the simplest example. Cyber-netic principles are used to consider ways in which the family has developed habits that tend to neutralise or stabilise any change. In the example of the anorectic girl, the father became depressed after his daughter was admitted to hospital and began to improve. Strains in the marriage appeared and the mother developed a number of hypochondriacal symptoms. The youngest sibling began to steal. The girl eventually became so worried about them all that she discharged herself from hospital and soon after resumed her fasting behaviour. The others then improved.

Thus, the behaviour of the members of the family could be seen as responding to a change (the young girl leaving home) whilst the effect of their behaviour was ultimately to maintain stability, albeit an inappropriate stability and at a high cost. It was from observations such as these that the term 'family homeostasis' was coined (Jackson, 1957).

Family Patterns and the 'Family Dance'

Imagine an event where you are sitting at dinner with some members of your family, say your parents if they are alive, or perhaps your children. Maybe there are others: grandparents, siblings, aunts, uncles or cousins. Imagine that a small and common or familiar conflict develops. Perhaps it starts with the question of who is to visit whom at the weekend, or some comment on your dress or diet. If you can imagine such a scene, you may be able to predict more or less accurately who would say what, roughly in what order, and the sort of tone with which each would speak. You may be able to go further. You may be able to predict to what degree of tension or passion the conflict will develop and two or three ways in which it will 'end'. What you will have remembered is an interactional sequence and one which is likely to be repeated with a similar shape and similar attitudes taken by the various members, despite the fact that the subject of conflict might differ markedly. I put the 'end' in inverted commas because, of course, it is not really the end. It is only the punctuation of a sequence which, together with other sequences, makes up the interactional pattern of the family. This sequence could 'end' with a senior member of the household perhaps looking stern, raising his voice, perhaps shouting, banging the table, perhaps threatening violence or perhaps carrying out violence. The amount of feeling and the level of conflict tolerated in different families will be idiosyncratic to that family. However, the ending of a sequence with one member taking a strong and challenging position is one pattern which will occur in many families in a predominantly patriarchal culture. In cultures with a different orientation to gender and power this may be different.

There are many alternative punctuations to such a sequence. It could end with somebody becoming upset, bursting into tears, leaving the room or the house, or with another member placating and 'calming things down'. It could end with a diversion: someone making a joke, an external intrusion such as the telephone or perhaps a child becoming excited or misbehaving. Diversion by a child is a common ending to such a sequence of conflict in many families. In some families, however, the child's over-reaction to increasing tension is in somatic form. If the child has a predisposition to asthma for example, the child is likely to have an asthma attack at times of high tension, particularly if this concerns the parents. Such an attack will often then divert attention from the conflict in the family, as members of the family cooperate to assist the afflicted member (Minuchin et al., 1978). At this point, the problem of considering causality can be seen. It could be said that the tension in the family precipitates the asthmatic attacks; alternatively, it could be said that the asthmatic attacks control tension in the family.

Short-term Pattern and Pattern over Time

If you were able to imagine a family sequence, then you could ask, 'Who made it happen?'. The answer has to be, 'Everyone present'. In fact, if the sequence was experienced as unpleasant, most members of the family would probably admit that they had individually resolved 'never to let it happen like that again'. Yet as soon as they are together, they will often repeat a similar set of sequences.

The kind of sequence, which I hope you have been able to illustrate from your own experience, might repeat many times over the course of a few hours or days. To refer to the family of the anorectic girl, a common sequence would be that Susan would return from school and suggest to her mother that she was going out. The mother would complain that she did not help in the house but not directly insist that Susan stay in. As tension developed between the mother and Susan, younger brother Ben would demonstrate his 'difference' from Susan by offering to help his mother and telling her many things about his school day. Susan would become increasingly angry and provocative in response to Ben's relationship with his mother, to the point where, on father's return, the mother would make demands on him to control Susan. Conflict would then escalate between mother and Susan which would be followed by the parents arguing with each other. The children would then fight and the parents would then interrupt their own argument to control the two children. This is quite a complicated sequence. In various similar forms it would repeat frequently, and it could be seen how the girl's symptom of not eating could easily take the place of the children's fighting, in interfering with the parents' arguments, albeit arguments which they might see as having been 'caused' by her.

However, there are more complex patterns which repeat much less frequently. For example, in some families, it can be observed that the mother and Susan remain on good terms, with father left out for approximately 2–3 months; perhaps this reverses, with father and Susan being close for a few weeks, after which mother and Susan are again close. The people in such a family know that each change is not really a 'change', but only a punctuation. There are perhaps also other sequences which repeat with much less frequency. It can often be noted that a particular set of behaviours occurs in one generation, misses a generation and then can be found between parents and child in the following generation.

The important point is that these patterns do not occur because somebody 'makes' them happen. Rather, thay are a function of the organization of relationships which has become set up in the family. We could postulate unconscious motives for each member which propagate such patterns, but an important aspect of these patterns is that *they provide the family with some stability*. Inasmuch as maintaining stability is often experienced by the members as a way of protecting the family and those in it, therefore, one function of such behaviour is to achieve a degree of *mutual protectiveness*.

Balance and Stability vs Change in the Family

The family is a context in which people live. These people are at different levels of development, physically and emotionally. For this development to progress, a certain degree of stability is necessary. At the same time, a certain degree of flexibility is necessary for the family to adapt, for example, to the children requiring more independence, privacy, autonomy etc. Thus, throughout all families, there is a constant tension between these contradictory forces for change and stability. Many problems can be understood in terms of the failure to resolve this conflict in the family or, put another way, that adaption has become incongruent to the current focus of development in the family whilst it may have been quite congruent to an earlier set of circumstances.

In the family of the anorectic girl, the various behaviours of the family members could be seen as accommodating to the change in such a way as to maintain temporarily the previous status quo. Several research projects, e.g. Mossige et al. (1979), have demonstrated that in families with a schizophrenic member there is a greater tendency, particularly in the case of the symptomatic member, for the individual opinions and perceptions to be modified to fit the 'orthodox family' opinion.

The work at the Philadelphia Child Guidance Clinic on what they term 'psychosomatic families' strongly supports the view that the illness in the child plays an important role in the regulation of conflict within the family. Their most dramatic study was to measure the free fatty acid (FFA) level of severely labile diabetic children and their parents during a standardised task interview (Minuchin et al., 1978). The free fatty acid level has been shown to rise in ketoacidosis, but is also a useful measure of emotional stress. The 'labile group' of diabetic children required hospitalisation for correction of acidosis as much as once a week. The child was initially left outside the room observing from behind a one-way mirror a family argument which the parents had been asked to solve. During this period, the free fatty acid in at least one of the parents would rise markedly while the level in the child would continue to rise slowly. The child was then brought into the room and the three of them were asked to help each other to resolve the argument. At this point the free fatty acid level in the parents markedly dropped whilst the FFA level in the child continued to rise more steeply, and it remained high after the end of the interview. Thus it would appear that the child's intervention actually lowered the level of stress in the parents.

The Question of Intervention

Despite the plethora of research, there are only very few controlled trials that successfully demonstrate the therapeutic efficacy of family therapy compared to other treatments. The best review of these is in the *Handbook of Family Therapy* by Gurman and Kniskern (1981). In the 'labile diabetics' referred to earlier, the re-hospitalisation rate dropped to almost nil after between 3 and 12 months' family therapy. Some very important work has been done by Leff and others (1982) which has conclusively demonstrated that the factor, 'Expressed Emotion', assessed in the relatives of schizophrenics can be a critical factor in forecasting the relapse rate of the patient. When the Expressed Emotion is high, the relapse rate may be over 90 per cent regardless of the drug therapy given, whilst if it is low this can be kept well below 22 per cent. The nature of this factor is not fully understood and research on the possible application of family therapy to reducing 'expressed emotion' is only just beginning. However, a recent study (Asen et al., 1990) has demonstrated that the factor is also a useful generic measure of family change.

As to the question of whether it is 'worth it', this is easier to answer. The important thing is that practitioners of family therapy can frequently observe important and significant changes occurring both in family organisation and in the patient's problem after only a few sessions. In addition, this may happen without the 'side effects' of the patient becoming dependent on the therapist or of the family believing the solution to be out of their hands. The idea of bringing the whole family together, with fantasies of terrible family dramas erupting, may be daunting for some practitioners. The practitioner may believe that he could make a mistake and be responsible for 'breaking up the family'. This is highly unlikely. One reason for this is suggested by the illustrations.

Throughout this chapter, there have been illustrations of the powerful forces for stabilisation occurring in all families, particularly in those families, that are having difficulty in managing developmental transitions.

Some Aspects of Family Therapy

The goals of family therapists will vary widely but, almost universally, they are concerned to create an event in which some new 'information' is put into the family. This information (Bateson, 1973) is not some new data or knowledge that can be read in a book, but needs to be a different way of perceiving the events of which family members complain. This may occur through the family members being helped to understand the origins of the problem, through trying to understand or sharing unconscious fantasies, but it is more likely to take place through a series of interactions occurring in the session which relabel what had recently happened in a different way. In essence, the therapist attempts to create a family event which may be familiar in many ways, but he uses his knowledge of family organisation to help the family resolve it or to end the sequence or 'dance' in a different way. By having a different experience, the family members may then experience differences in perception of events that had previously been felt as unpleasant exchanges. For example, in one family in which there was a 16-year-old deaf daughter, and a 12-year-old boy who was not attending school and had been defined by the family as 'retarded', the mother complained that the whole load of worry about the family fell on her shoulders. Both she and her husband seemed to agree that the husband was 'distant, detached and disinterested'. The therapist suspected that this was a collusive relationship, i.e. he believed that the mother and the children (and the father as well) were all behaving in a way that kept the mother over-burdened and kept the father distant. The therapist believed that this view of the family was inefficient and was playing an important part in keeping the young boy behaving much less competently than he was able. In order to change this view of the roles of the mother and father, the therapist needed first to challenge the idea of the father being distant and secondly almost to stage-manage an event in which he and the mother begin to play their customary parts. An example of challenging the idea of the father being distant was initiated by the therapist asking the father how his wife had coped when she realised her first child was deaf. The father answered that 'it took its toll'. The therapist pressed the father as to whom the mother had gained her support from: had it been from the children, had it been from her mother or had it been from him? The father answered, 'I don't know'.

From the way the family had been describing the father, the therapist could have predicted that the mother and father would 'agree' that this was because the father was disinterested. The therapist, however, defined the situation differently.

> Therapist: 'It sounds like she does not tell you much about what she is thinking'.
> Father: 'Probably not.'
> Therapist: 'So you seem to get left out quite a lot.'
> Father: 'No.'
> Mother: 'No, he likes to be left out.'
> The therapist now begins to challenge this definition.
> Therapist to father: 'Just a minute. Is this really true?'
> Father: 'I do, yes.'
> Therapist: 'Ah, but who sold you the idea?'

The therapist continues to take this position until eventually the father responds by acknowledging that he actually finds it very difficult to play an active part in the family as he feels his wife has already decided everything. Which of these definitions of the father is 'true' is not that relevant. The importance is that the therapist has opened up an alternative way of viewing things. This couple were unaccustomed to continuing their disagreements to a point of resolution. Commonly, disagreements would end by the mother taking a decision, or by the children providing a diversion. In the presence of the therapist, both partners turned to him with their point of view, assuming that he would resolve the disagreement. It is at this point that the therapist has the opportunity deliberately to provoke an event which ends in an unfamiliar way for the family. That is that the couple begin to face and resolve their differences.

> Therapist: 'No! Sort it out together!' (To the wife) 'With him! *He's* your husband, not me!'
> The mother finally turns to the father and complains.
> Mother: 'I took Ben to the doctor's. I tried to get it all straightened out. You just spoke about it, but I did it.'
> Father: 'Right.'
> Therapist to father: 'Go on.'
> Father: 'No, no, no.'

At this point, the therapist challenges the position the father is taking by defining him as compliant rather than as disinterested. The therapist asks the father, 'So is this what happens at home? She makes a speech and you say right?'. The therapist presses this issue until eventually the father confronts the mother with the fact that he feels unable to stand up to her as she is always much more verbal than he, so he eventually 'gives up and ignores her'. Subsequently, the couple begin to experiment with an alternative way of responding to each other, particularly in relation to their roles as parents. In doing this, the therapist has temporarily increased the level of conflict beyond the level which usually occurs in the family. The goal is not so much to help them to understand the conscious or unconscious 'reason' for their difficulties, but rather to experience a different view of their relationship so that they can begin to respond to the children and each other differently.

In general, family therapists would not see interpretation as a useful way of introducing this information. However, consider the following sequence:

> A young girl of 11 is brought by her mother and step-father with the complaint that she is constantly crying. Her mother has complained that at times she has felt like strangling her and there was a time when she threatened to have her taken into care.

There were in the session two younger brothers who tended to observe in a rather distant way the interaction between Pamela and her mother. It is, however, significant that Pamela was nearing the age of 12, and it had not been acknowledged that the mother had had two previous families by different men. In both cases, the mother had left, or the family had broken up when the eldest reached the age of 12. In the third of the five sessions for which the family were seen, Pamela is fingering a little box, looking away and generally refusing to speak. The excerpt illustrates the interaction of the therapist, girl and family around the box, and the therapist's response.

Therapist: 'You keep showing that to me. It must be very important. What is it?'
Girl: 'It is a box.'
Therapist: 'Can I have a look? I feel I am supposed to see it. Am I allowed to look inside or don't you want to show it to me?'
Mother: 'I don't think there is anything in it, is there?'
Therapist: 'You decide, Pamela, is it private?'
Mother: 'It is all the silly things she brought out with her.'
Therapist: 'The family think it is all rubbish; is that right?'
Father: 'It is not rubbish, just her own things.'
Therapist: 'Yes, private things?'
Father: 'They are not really private, they are what girls of her age collect.'
Girl pulls out broken bracelet and other broken trinkets from the box.
Therapist: 'I think it is very important that you carry all the different bits and pieces that are broken and keep them with you and look after them and that is rather like what my colleague thought Pamela is doing for the family; that she was doing some crying, that we didn't really understand what the crying was about yet, but carrying some of the broken things, things that have got broken in the past for the family and that that is why it was so unbearable for the family because she was carrying in her all these hurts and broken things which really you must have felt as well.'

In this example, a piece of behaviour is interpreted to represent an unconscious expression of a family dilemma. It is not suggested that this link is 'true' or 'untrue' but rather that it has a useful function if it links in the girl's behaviour with that of the rest of the family.

Another Clinical Example

The following case illustrates:

1. The tension between stability and change.
2. The intensity and repetitiveness of the sequences and patterns in the family: 'the family dance'.
3. The impact of change in the wider system (retirement and the stabilising effect of the day hospital treatment).
4. The case therefore illustrates also the intervention of the family therapist in the wider system of family and professional.

> Wendy was an only child, aged 20 when referred. Her mother, Anne, had not known her own mother and had been brought up by an aunt and her grandmother. She was nervous when she had Wendy and this was aggravated when the paediatrician suggested that Wendy may be partially sighted. This later turned out to be untrue, but it was one factor which pushed Wendy and her mother closer together in the first few years. Another factor was that the father Simon, aged 60, was often away. He had recently retired from an active life as an officer in the army. He had had long periods away from home on

missions to which his family either could not, or had chosen not to, follow him. Wendy and her mother continued to live in Scotland. Simon's retirement almost coincided with the time when Wendy would be leaving school and perhaps leaving home.

Eighteen months before referral to the family therapy clinic Wendy had been attending a day hospital run for the armed forces near her home in Scotland. She had been 'unable' to work because of 'obsessional rituals'. These involved washing and, most specifically, clothes washing rituals. She claimed that these were caused by 'contaminations', which she experienced in crowded places, particularly in two nearby towns where there happened to be many young soldiers, but also if accidentally touched by either of her parents. At home she was perceived by her parents, and behaved, as irritatingly incompetent. She would insist that her parents help her with any activity, writing a letter, filling the washing machine etc. In the day hospital she attended groups with other patients, had the almost full attention of one senior nurse, spent 2 hours a week with her psychiatrist and was particularly attached to her psychologist. The latter had attempted several behavioural training programmes with frustrating results. The family was seen for some 17 sessions during the course of 2½ years. These sessions began on a weekly basis. In the first session the therapist noted that as they came into the room the parents motioned Wendy where to sit, then they suggested which clothes she should remove for comfort and watched her anxiously if she was asked any questions, clearly ready with the 'correct' reply. Wendy, in the first session, found it almost impossible to say anything on her own behalf. She expected her parents to speak for her or that the therapist could rely on the report received from the other psychiatrists, nurses, psychologists etc. The therapist chose to ignore the parents and repeatedly asked Wendy 'why had she come?'. Finally, and with great difficulty, she was able to say, 'It's because of the crossed wires'.

In this first session it was clear that the family organisation was one that supported Wendy remaining incompetent. This then brought the parents together in their relatively new role as shared parents (the father recently having retired). Wendy was now behaving in a way which was appropriate to a much younger child. The therapist began to challenge the parents' interruptions, observed the way in which Wendy would 'activate' them to speak and blocked this behaviour. Gradually, Wendy began to take on more responsibility at home, but despite this continued to attend the day hospital. The therapist realised that the latter was providing Wendy with a life which was richer than anything she could conceive of outside. Having no siblings and no friends, she had little impetus for change. The therapist asked her whether her parents would welcome the effect on her which more independence would bring (such as speaking up for herself more clearly, taking a more independent line etc.). To the great surprise and shock of her parents she answered, 'No, I don't think they are ready, I think they would prefer me to remain a baby'. The therapist suggested that perhaps the day hospital was a good solution for everyone. It allowed the parents to continue to feel they were doing the 'right thing' by their daughter and it allowed Wendy to have a life, apparently as an adult, while in reality she was treated as a child. The therapist suggested that maybe this is what they should settle for and prescribed caution about any abrupt change. The goal of this was to face Wendy and her parents with a different framework – for thinking about her symptoms – as representing a 'costly' (in terms of lost life opportunities) solution to a real dilemma which they all shared. He left the family without offering another appointment. Two weeks later the therapist received a letter from Wendy, the first that she had written herself, saying that she had disharged herself from the day hospital and would like another consultation for the family. The therapist had realised that two aspects of the wider system were playing an important part in Wendy's problems; the father's retirement from an institution on which he was highly dependent (the army), and Wendy's involvement in an institution on which she was highly dependent (the day hospital), the staff of which the therapist believed responded with anxiety whenever she made a bid for more independence. It was relatively useless to challenge the repetitive family sequences without also addressing the stabilising effects of the wider system. Thus, by suggesting that the family settle for the status quo with Wendy remaining as a patient in the day hospital, the therapist had forced both Wendy and her parents to face their conflict about change and to make a real choice. From this point on, therapy moved more quickly but, after discharge from the day hospital, Wendy complained more acutely of her 'contaminations'. The therapist suggested that the family should not attempt to 'cure' these, but rather they should think of them as a problem of loneliness, i.e. that 'nobody could understand just exactly what Wendy felt like when having these feelings'. He therefore asked Wendy if she would agree to her parents making these feelings worse so that she could describe them with more passion and the parents could understand them more fully. He therefore asked the parents to push Wendy into crowded places and touch her whenever possible, for one week. The parents were amazed when Wendy agreed to this, as they had always avoided confrontation with her and accommodated her every request. The mother then acknowledged that she had a phobia about cats and the father and Wendy agreed to bring cats into the house to do the same thing for her. Finally, the father acknowledged that he had a phobia of heights and the mother and Wendy agreed to take the father for a walk along the nearby cliffs. This session ended with great jocularity and on their return, not surprisingly, they had been unable to elicit the expected symptoms in any of these situations. Thus, the symptoms had ceased to have a stabilising influence in the family and had become part of a more playful behaviour which allowed more freedom and experimentation.

Later aspects of the therapy were concerned with helping Wendy to think about how to get a job without her parents doing it for her, helping the mother to take charge of the father, so that he became less anxious and therefore less intrusive on Wendy and, finally, helping Wendy independently to leave home and find her own lodgings. Only then was she able to make friends and develop her own life.

In this case, the initial interventions were of a type described as direct intervention in the process of the session. However, the intervention which prescribed that Wendy should remain in the day hospital as a fitting solution to her and her parents' requirements of each other was designed to offer the family a caricature of an aspect of their shared perceptions of each other and one which was not previously acknowledged. This rather exaggerated portrayal created a crisis which allowed Wendy to leave the hospital and she and her parents to begin to be more courageous in facing issues of change.

Different Methods of Therapy with the Family

The kind of direct approach described in the second example does rely on the family members making an alliance for family change with the therapist. This, in turn, requires that the pressures for stability are not so great that the opportunities for change cannot be welcomed. When the family is thoroughly entrenched in a particular pattern, the members may be at a loss to experiment with alternatives or may see any alternative as a great threat.

In these situations, it is common for the therapist to adopt a more 'strategic' approach which often uses tasks that are not obviously directed towards change or may even be apparently prescribing what is already happening (Haley, 1977). The most coherent body of such work has been developed by the Centre for Family Studies in Milan (Pallazzoli et al., 1978). There is not, however, space in this chapter for further elaboration of this approach. Other approaches particularly explore the intergenerational patterns running through the family and may involve grandparents and extended family members in exploring these. The goal of this is to help the family members to feel less 'programmed' and more able to take autonomous decisions.

What is common in all the approaches, however, is that in general the therapist is less concerned with pathology and with dysfunction, and more concerned with blocking dysfunction and encouraging the discovery of latent or new repertoires of behaviour in the family.

Family Therapy, Group Psychotherapy and Individual Therapy

The last sections gave a taste of the operation of family therapy. Particularly in the first example, the therapist attempted to achieve small changes in sequence or pattern in the session as they occurred. Naturally, such small changes are not lasting, unless they are repeated with sufficient intensity and frequency that they become part of a new folklore in the family. Only at this point can such changes be generalised from the specific issues under discussion to other aspects of family life, so that there can be a real shift in the organisation of the family. This is quite different from the approach of other psychotherapies, detailed elsewhere in this volume. At this point it may be useful to clarify some of the differences between what the author has called family or 'natural' group therapy, in comparison with 'stranger' group therapy (i.e. when the group is formed from strangers for the purpose of therapy) and with individual psychotherapy. These are summarised in Table 8.1.

Impacts of Race, Ethnicity and Social Disadvantage

Some would argue that race and ethnicity should play no special part in the principles of therapeutic intervention. They would argue that people are people the world over, and stress that *they* are not prejudiced. Most employers, doctors, teachers, police or members of the judiciary would similarly protest their lack of racial discrimination. At the same time it is known that blacks are much less likely to be appointed to senior jobs, that they are much more likely to be hospitalised as psychotic, that they do much less well in the educational system despite comparable levels of intelligence, and they are much less likely to be granted bail while on remand than are whites for the same crimes. The staff of the Marlborough Family Service noticed that blacks and other ethnic minorities made proportionately much less use of our service, whilst often having as many or more problems for which we thought we could be potentially useful. Clearly, in all these situations some subtle process must be operating which acts to discriminate unfairly against ethnic minority groups, but the professional staff who participate in that same process may be partly or wholly unaware of it. Such a process has sometimes been called institutionalised racism.

The staff team of the Marlborough Family Service decided to employ black consultants to provide anti-racist training for the whole group in an attempt to ensure that the service served equally all ethnic groups in the community. In the follow-up to that training, we began to look at our building, literature,

Table 8.1 Comparison between family group therapy, 'stranger' group therapy and individual therapy

Individual therapy	'Stranger' group therapy	Natural (family) group therapy
The patient/therapist relationship exists only as a context for therapy	The group exists only as a context for therapy	The family has a life of its own, with a history and an anticipated future
Therapy occurs in the context of the intensity of relationship between therapist and patient	Therapy occurs in the context of the intensity of relationships between the therapist and group members, and between group members	Therapy occurs in context of a change in relationship pattern in the context of the current intense family relationships
Thus – the therapist is central	Thus – at different times the therapist or some part of the group may be central	Thus – the therapist is principally an agent of change rather than a central actor
The therapist *allows* the intensity of affect from the patient to him or her to develop (although the setting may provoke it)	The therapist facilitates the 'integration' or 'gelling' of the group in the service of therapy	The therapist is more likely to be concerned to develop the differentiation of the group
Therapist and patient maintain a non-social relationship (to varying degrees depending on the model)	The members are discouraged from meeting between sessions	The members remain in an intense relationship between sessions
The therapist does not try to develop structure in the therapeutic relationship, and interpretations may be used to highlight inappropriate structural patterns sought by the patient. In child psychotherapy the therapist *may* be forced to be a parental adult	There is no permanent structural organisation of the group. That which evolves is transient and often seen by the therapist as a recreation of past or 'inner' families of the members. The members are usually of similar age, as may be the therapist. The therapist aims to be 'meta' to the group	The family has an inherent and necessary hierarchical organisation, relating to the different ages, developmental positions and responsibilities of the members. As the therapist is an adult, this will affect how he or she is used by the family. The therapist aims to *think* from a meta-position, but may *act* in a partisan manner
Change occurs through understanding the meaning of an old pattern in a new context. This change has then to be generalised to other contexts. The pattern in the original context may or *may not* change	Change occurs through understanding the meaning of an old pattern in a new context. This change has then to be generalised to other contexts. The pattern in the original context may or *may not* change	Change occurs through changing the pattern in an 'old' context, so that the context itself is changed

language, in fact all our practices, in terms of what would make them more friendly to ethnic minorities. One of the practices we began to adopt was to talk to the family about their feelings about having a white therapist, when they must have experienced discriminatory relationships with other white professionals who may have been in positions of relative power in relation to them. We would further point out that they could not as yet be sure we would not behave similarly. I had been working with a young couple in which the husband, Rajiv, was of Indian Hindu background. His father had brought the family to Britain after the Tanzanian government introduced discriminatory legislation against the employment of Asians in academic jobs. He was married to a French woman and they had one child of three. They were both well educated. Although, when I first saw them he was unemployed, they could not have been described as obviously socially disadvantaged. Three months later he had been asked to run an engineering firm. A year later it was expanding fast. The problem the wife, Odette, complained of was that after he had had an affair, he had become obsessed with work and never listened to her. He complained that she was depressed and depressing, as well as sexually restrictive. When she was pregnant with her second child these problems exacerbated; she considered an abortion but instead they consulted me again. When I saw them he told me that Odette was always complaining that his mind was never with her and that she would speak and he would not hear her. I imagined the voices of my team asking, 'Why are you not discussing the racial issue with this man?'. In my head my voice answered that with this middle-class successful man it would be insulting; after all he is so 'British'. The voices continued to argue with me. He was telling me about the problems of relocating his factory, and there was something in his description which led me to wonder why he was moving from one part of the country to another. My team won and I rather clumsily asked whether there was some racial prejudice issue in this move, and that he had never even acknowledged his racial difference, so perhaps he thought I would be prejudiced against him in favour of Odette. He was extremely surprised and relieved by this statement, said he had never talked to anybody about his race, including Odette. When the family had emigrated to England his father had moved from an academic job to a lowly manual one, and he blamed this for his father later becoming depressed and alcoholic. He had bitterly despised his father's reaction, and vowed never to allow himself to be in a situation in which he was vulnerable and could be humiliated. This explained the move, as he felt the community in which his factory was placed to be prejudiced against him because of his colour, but had not been able to say this to Odette. He then linked this to the way he kept aloof from Odette.

The result of this initially uncomfortable conversation was that we broke a taboo – one that had been operating on me as well as on him. Having broken it, however, he was left in some sense vulnerable in relation to me – perhaps before he was ready. One practice the team had recently developed was to try and find some area of life that can be shared by therapist and family or patient, and that can cut across the differences in terms of culture and power. Actually, I was not thinking of this but he kept talking of the way he absolutely could not hear Odette when he was so obsessed by work. I told him that the only real time I had that experience was when I was working on my wind generators. He said 'What!'. I told him of the three wind-driven electric generators I had developed. I would often go there to work with them or play with them, which involved working up a 10 metre pole. At these times I was exactly like him, and could hear nobody, but I added that it was more limited and pleasurable. The next time he came with Odette he brought a design for a new wind generator with a cordless motor that he was considering developing.

Thus, through the process of my eventual challenge of what had become a shared taboo subject, and through one might say accidentally discovering an area of mutual interest, both he and I were freed of some unhelpful constraints. The result was that he was then able to use the consultation to examine some incongruent aspects of his adaptation to the host culture. This, in turn, led to a more mutually respectful debate by the couple about the management of their family life.

This vignette illustrates how therapist's and family members' feelings about race can lead to realistic mistrust of the therapist, with consequent interference with his or her usefulness to the family. Rajiv, however, had much in common with the therapist in terms of social class and interests. An even greater sensitivity and a greater effort to connect is called for when the family is also socially disadvantaged through, for example, poverty.

Ayo was aged 34, and the mother of two boys, Alex, aged 13, and Jason, aged 11. The boys were by two different fathers, and had both been made Wards of Court in infancy on the basis of injuries received from Jason's father. The two boys had been placed in long-term foster care with different foster parents. Ayo, however, had never accepted this, and had fought hard to get her children back. She had kept in as much contact with them as the Social Services would allow, and several years ago had used the Marlborough Family Service Intensive Treatment Programme as a way of being united with Alex, as a result of which he was eventually returned to her care. The situation with Jason had been a bit more difficult. Jason was fostered to a family in the country, in a community and culture that was totally different to that of his original family, and quite different from that in which he would live in London. Ayo, however, was determined to get him back and complied with every possible ruling made by the Social Services Department. She now had a stable boyfriend called Fred, who had made a good relationship with Alex. In a family meeting in which all members of the family (including the grandfather and Fred) were present it became clear that there was some kind of, but unspecified, problem about Jason returning. Jason was a lively intelligent and outspoken young man. I began to realise that Fred was not sure if he had Ayo's permision to say what was on his mind. I raised the question as to whether there was not some racial issue about the way in which Jason had been brought up, but that Fred would assume that I would be on the 'side' of the foster parents. Eventually, after considerable uneasiness, Fred explained that he was worried that Jason would get into trouble with the police in the area where they lived, as he was too 'trustful'. If he was going to survive 'in our area' he would have to learn to mistrust the police and all 'white' authorities and to avoid contact with them. It transpired that each member of the family had tried to say this to Jason in different ways, but had been so worried about saying it aloud that they had not acknowledged it to each other. I pointed out that they had no certainty about my trustworthiness either, and we would have to discuss how they were going to deal with that. After many reassurances to me that I was 'OK' Ayo eventually admitted that she felt she must hide from me any potential problems about Jason returning or she would lose her fight to get him back. She then acknowledged that she had believed that the two children had been made Wards of Court without any other options being considered, and that she believed this was because of her being black. Once all of this had been acknowledged, and the therapist had recognised the bad relationship between the police and the black community in their neighbourhood, the family was able to plan much more realistically for Jason's return home.

We can and should expect people in such circumstances to be appropriately suspicious and mistrustful. It is then important for the practitioner not to interpret this as pathology, but to find a way of acknowledging the disadvantage faced by the family, while also encouraging them to see the aspects of this disadvantage which they can realistically fight. The practitioner also needs to show respect for the successful ways they have managed despite these extra burdens.

Applications to Different Kinds of Family Structure and 'Non-family' Human Systems

An obvious question is: for what diagnostic categories is family therapy applicable? The goal of family therapy is not to remove a 'cause', but rather to interfere with patterns which maintain a problem and to promote the development of more healthy patterns. This can be applied in any context where such an agreement can be worked out, and yet it has been found to be a particularly potent form of therapy in the behavioural and psychosomatic disorders of children, in neurotic and relationship problems in adults and in substance abuse. In addition, it has been used with the families of schizophrenics, particularly those in the process of rehabilitation, and in families where there is a seriously ill or dying member, or the consequences of a recent bereavement.

The model of family on which the illustrations have been based, for convenience rather than for truth, has been that of the traditional white, western European nuclear family. Many people, however, do not live in the tidy group of 2 parents and 2.4 children and in many cultures this is not the traditional structure. Three family structures are of particular importance:

1. Single parent families, whether as a result of divorce, bereavement or the lack of a partner.
2. Extended family organisations as, for example, when a young couple or a single parent live with their parents, perhaps siblings, other family members, and other co-opted family members.
3. Remarried families, sometimes called blended families or reconstituted families.

For each of these three structures, there are particular issues which the therapist needs to be aware of and incorporate in his or her views concerning intervention. In the single parent family, the parent needs more support and non-family social contacts take on greater significance. However, the parent's authority may have to be more autocratic, or he or she may need to delegate authority to the elder siblings. It is easy to see what can go wrong when an elder sibling takes authority unilaterally. Alternatively, if a parent responds to the loneliness of being single by befriending the children, he or she may then be unable to help them make the necessary developmental transitions.

In the extended family organisation, there is a particular danger of confusion between the roles of parents and grandparents. For example, will the grandparents' support be seen as underpinning or undermining the parents' authority, and how can the parent help the grandparent find a useful role which is not in competition with him or her? In addition, the children and the grandparent may be allied against the parent. In a positive way, this may allow the child freedom of access to someone with whom they are less emotionally involved, but in a negative way it may be perceived by the parent as 'stealing their child'. However, in some Indian, Chinese, and other cultures, it may be mutually expected that the grandparents would retain primacy of influence.

In the remarried family, all these issues are still poignant, but in addition:

1. The problem of the children resolving the conflict of loyalty between the step-parent and the absent parent continues to be an issue and it depends particularly on the degree to which, for example, the divorced couple are still fighting or have accepted the new liaison.
2. There is also the problem of the children having changed their 'position' in the family. Thus, an elder child in the original family may have

half-brothers or -sisters who are older, and find him- or herself becoming the younger child or vice versa.

Each different structure has its own strengths and weaknesses in terms of the goal of promoting the development of the children. The job for the family therapist is first to understand the organisation and structure in which the people live, and secondly to plan his or her interventions on the basis of what is most functional for that family at that time. For example, in the single parent family, it may be appropriate to encourage the mother to rely more on an elder sibling for certain functions such as helping with the younger children. In another family, this may have happened to a degree where the elder sibling is in competition with her. In the latter case, she may need to be helped to re-establish her authority so that an appropriate generational boundary develops between her and the elder child.

Thus, the task for the therapist is to think about the organisation and functioning of the system and to use him- or herself to create a new balance in the dilemma between stability and change. This thinking can then be applied to a child living in a children's home, to a school classroom situation or, with certain modifications, to a social delivery agency or even an industrial organisation.

What can the Practitioner do?

The training of nearly all practitioners, whether in medicine, psychology or social work, has underlined the individual integrity of the patient. This chapter has been about seeing the patient as part of a wider system, the family and 'others', and seeing his or her problems as, in part, a manifestation of those relationships.

The author would like to feel that this chapter has introduced the practitioner to the process of thinking in terms of relationships, rather than cause, and to consider the whole system rather than just its parts. I hope it has also illustrated how the family therapist can use this thinking to engage actively in the processes of the family. Of course, he or she is then also *part* of the system which is struggling between stability and change. To a degree, all therapists and practitioners are part of the system which they treat. This was well illustrated in the case of Wendy and her therapist in the day hospital as well as in the case in which the therapist had to make an ethnic bridge with the patient. The author hopes that the practitioner will be stimulated to think how to increase the competence in the family rather than the incompetence. *As well as thinking of the consequences* of giving a remedy such as tranquillisers, the practitioner might anticipate the effects for the whole system of *not* giving a remedy. Lastly, I hope I have demonstrated that the practitioner may need to develop and maintain a quite different perspective from that held by the family members, and to think how to engender a different set of perceptions in those who are concerned to achieve a change. I have also described in some detail some of the forces in a family which tend towards the maintenance of stability. It is therefore not surprising that when a practitioner offers what he or she thinks are rational solutions, they are frequently not welcomed as warmly as might be hoped. In fact, to get through this, the practitioner may often need to think of solutions which are quite 'irrational' in everyday terms. One such solution was used in the case of Wendy.

However, this chapter has not provided a recipe of how to 'do family therapy'. Learning from the written word has severe limitations in acquiring any active skill. In the final section some useful reading is listed, as well as more useful suggestions as to how the practitioner can acquire skill in understanding and intervening in families.

Further Reading and Opportunities for Learning and Training

For those who want to read further I would suggest the simplest book is *Working with Families* by Gill Gorell Barnes (1984). There is also a selection of papers published in the *Journal of The Royal Society of Medicine* (1985) on family work in general practice. Perhaps the clearest exposition is in three books by Salvador Minuchin; the first is *Families and Family Therapy* (Minuchin, 1974); the second is *Psychosomatic Families* (Minuchin et al., 1978); and the most recent is *Family Therapy Techniques* (Minuchin and Fishman, 1981). For a clearer exposition of a slightly different, but related, approach, I would recommend reading *Problem Solving Therapy* by Jay Haley (1977).

However, the best way for the practitioner to develop some skills is to join up with one or more colleagues, who have decided to explore their thinking and work with families. They can use discussion, observe each other's work, perhaps play tape recordings, or arrange sessions together and consult each other. The forming of such a group can allow the development of the inventiveness and imagination of the members, essential ingredients for working with families. Details of how to carry out this kind of consultation/supervision are also the subject of many of the courses which are provided by the institutions listed below. Information on conferences, a journal and local courses are available from the Association for Family Therapy, 6 Heol Seddon, Danes Court, Llandaff, Cardiff CF5 2QX. In recent years, the British Postgraduate Medical Federation has run courses for general practitioners, and there are courses run at independent institutes in London (The Institute of Family Therapy, 43 New Cavendish Street, London W1, Tel: 071–935 1651), and Cardiff (The Family Institute, 15 Cathedral Road, Cardiff, Tel: 0222–28747).

There are also courses run at Newcastle Polytechnic and at the University of Birmingham, in Bristol, North Wales and Manchester as well as Scotland and Ireland. Lists of organisations providing these and other courses are available from the Association for Family Therapy.

References

ASEN, K., BERKOWITZ, R., COOKLIN, A.I. et al. (1991). Family therapy outcome research: a trial for families, therapists and researchers. *Family Process* in press.

ASHBY, W.R. (1956). *Introduction to cybernetics*. New York: John Wiley.

BATESON, G. (1973). *Steps towards an ecology of mind*. St Albans: Paladin.

BERTALANFFY, L. VON (1968). *General System Theory*. New York: Brazillier.

COOKLIN, A.I. (1973). Consideration of the 'contract' between staff and patient and its relationship to current hospital practice. *British Journal of Medical Psychology* **45**, 279–285.

GORELL BARNES, G. (1984). *Working with Families*. London: Macmillan/BASW.

GURMAN, A.S. and KNISKERN, D.P. (1981). *Handbook of Family Therapy*. New York: Brunner/Mazel.

HALEY, J. (1977). *Problem Solving Therapy*. California: Jossey-Bass.

JACKSON, D.D. (1957). The question of family homeostasis. *Psychiatry Quarterly Supplement* **31**, 79–80.

LEFF, J., KUIPERS, L., BERKOWITZ, R. et al. (1982). A controlled trial of social intervention in the families of schizophrenic patients. *British Journal of Psychiatry* **141**, 121–134.

MINUCHIN, S. (1974). *Families and Family Therapy*. London: Tavistock Publications.

MINUCHIN, S., ROSMAN, B. and BAKER, L. (1978). *Psychosomatic Families*. Cambridge, MA: Harvard University Press.

MINUCHIN, S. and FISHMAN, C. (1981). *Family Therapy Techniques*. Cambridge, MA: Harvard University Press.

MOSSIGE, S., PETTERSON, R.B. and BLAKER, R.M. (1979). Egocentrism and inefficiency in the communication of families containing a schizophrenic member. *Family Process* **18**, 405–425.

PALLAZZOLI, M.S., BOSCOLO L., CECCHIN, G. and PRATA, G. (1978). *Paradox and Counter Paradox: A New Model in the Therapy of the Family in Schizophrenic Transaction*. London: Jason Aronson.

ROYAL SOCIETY OF MEDICINE (1985). Selected papers on family work in general practice. *Journal of the Royal Society of Medicine* **78** (8).

Chapter 9
Behaviour Therapy

ALAN KING

Although behaviour therapy is a relatively straightforward form of psychological treatment an adequate definition of it is, necessarily, rather lengthy. Unlike most other forms of psychotherapy it cannot be entirely defined on the basis of theory. Its effects, and various phenomena which have been observed during research into behaviour therapy, have been partially explained in terms of learning theory which derives from the work of Pavlov and of Skinner into classical and operant conditioning. Learning theory has not, however, proved to be a perfect model. In fact, the techniques which so characterise behaviour therapy are used not because their effect has been predicted according to theory, but because experience has demonstrated it. Furthermore, many of the techniques of modern behaviour therapy can be traced back to methods of treatment described in medical writings which long predate the evolution of learning theory. Behaviour therapy, therefore, is essentially *empirical* rather than theoretical and is best defined in descriptive terms.

Just as characteristic as its techniques, with their emphasis upon overt behaviour, is the particular approach which behaviour therapy takes towards clinical problems. In contrast to other forms of psychotherapy, which seek to examine the historical antecedents of a problem, behaviour therapy is *symptom oriented*. As far as the behaviourist is concerned symptoms include not only the subjective experiences that tell us that we are unwell, but inappropriate behaviours, disturbing thoughts and abnormal emotional states. Behaviour therapy is directed towards the relief of these symptoms and this has made it relatively easy to establish specific therapeutic goals, a feature which gives behaviour therapy some of its structure. This is reinforced by the use of written or verbal contracts and by the application of specified *time limits* which are negotiated before treatment begins. Time limiting a teatment programme is possible because behavioural treatments tend to be *short term* so that the likely duration of therapy can be predicted. The precise duration of treatment is variable, depending upon the condition which is being treated, but six to ten sessions represent an average therapeutic investment. The therapist's style is outstandingly *directive* rather than reflective or interpretive and he or she, as well as the subject, takes an *active* role in treatment, with *collaboration* between them being an intrinsic feature of the process.

Behaviour therapy has been applied with varying degrees of success in a wide range of disorders and new applications continue to be disovered. As far as its *clinical uses* are concerned, there is a spectrum of therapeutic styles which reflects differences in the various problems it is used to treat, and in the clientèle which presents them. On one hand, the subject who has a neurotic disorder tends to be well motivated for change through treatment. He is usually his own advocate and, as well as a behavioural component, his complaint includes physical and emotional symptoms which are causing him distress. By contrast, the subject in an institution for the chronically mentally disordered is generally poorly motivated for change. Usually, the complaint is made by a member of staff and is confined specifically to the subject's behaviour. These differences require rather distinct therapeutic approaches.

In the management of neurosis, negotiation and explanation are fundamental features. Therapy is client directed, the subject is responsible for seeing through his or her own programme and the observations by which progress is judged are based mainly upon his or her own subjective experience and personal records. However, although the results that can be achieved using operant methods in the management of the chronically mentally disordered do appear to improve if effective negotiation and explanation are possible, these features are rather less important here than they are in the treatment of neurosis. At the same time, the subject's conscious cooperation and collaboration tend to be equally less crucial. Finally, operant programmes are under the control of staff who also carry out the observations and data recording by which treatment progress is measured.

Behaviour Therapy in the Neuroses

Assessment

Identification of the problem is the first task. Depending upon whose opinion is asked, there may be several views about what constitutes the problem. Initially, at least, the subject's own view, defined as clearly and as free from jargon as possible, is the one which is adopted. Alternatives are recorded and introduced later if necessary. A full psychiatric assessment will identify important aspects, such as current life stresses and any coexisting physical or psychiatric disorder that may influence a behavioural treatment.

Details of past and present treatment may suggest interventions that are likely to prove effective and the assessment is not complete without some enquiry into the use of alcohol and tranquillisers, both of which can interfere with some forms of behavioural treatment.

The rest of the assessment, called a *functional* or *behavioural* analysis, is characteristic of the behavioural approach. This consists of a highly detailed account of the current determinants of the problem rather than of its historical antecedents. Predisposing factors, such as heredity or early formative experiences, indicate why the subject should develop this particular problem and not another. Precipitating factors, such as major life events, tell us why the problem should develop when it did. Behaviour therapy, however, is interested in a third group – the perpetuating factors. These are the 'here and now' reasons why the problem has continued long after the precipitating factors have ceased to exert their effect. If the perpetuating factors can be overcome then the problem ought to improve.

The analysis is made easier by examining the perpetuating factors under three headings (Figure 9.1): the 'As', 'Bs' and the 'Cs'.

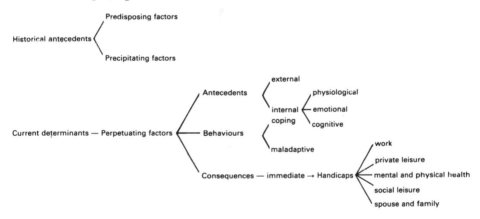

Figure 9.1   The functional analysis of the problem

The antecedents ('As')

The antecedents, or cues, may be external or internal. External cues include objects, situations, animals or people which immediately evoke the subject's symptoms. If these symptoms can be reproduced during the assessment session, either by introducing a relevant cue or by instructing the subject to carry out a simple manoeuvre such as overbreathing, immediate access is gained to the second group of cues. Internal cues are (1) physical, such as the bodily experiences that result from the physiological accompaniments of anxiety, (2) emotional, such as the fear experienced by phobic subjects and (3) cognitive, such as the disturbing thoughts and images that are so much a part of neurotic disorders.

The behaviours ('Bs')

These are the subject's overt responses. Those which maintain and strengthen the problem also restrict the subject's life in some way. They include avoidance, escape behaviours and ritualistic behaviours such as checking, cleaning and repeating. Sometimes the subject has discovered ways of coping with her problem such that the restrictions to her life are minimised. One of the tasks of treatment may be to improve upon these at the same time as overcoming the maladaptive behaviours by which the subject's life is handicapped.

The consequences ('Cs')

Although the subject's response to his discomfort has the effect or relieving it, this occurs at the *price* of ever-increasing restrictions to his life. In addition, maladaptive behaviours are reinforced by the very fact that they relieve discomfort immediately. The problem may be made worse by the efforts of family and friends who, in their desire to be of help and to deal with the problem, inadvertently reinforce it.

Eventually, as the disorder develops, immediate restrictions become major handicaps which are commonly the reasons why professional help is sought. Important areas of life which are affected include work, personal leisure, domestic functioning and interpersonal relationships. As well as causing handicaps in just those areas that will later provide an arena for the subject to tackle his or her problem, neurotic disorders cause secondary handicaps in other areas of life which may not be directly related to the initial problem.

Preparing for treatment

By ensuring that the subject fully understands the principles and implications of behaviour therapy and that he knows what is likely to be expected of him in treatment, the therapist is able to maximise the chances that treatment will be accepted and minimise the risk of sibsequent drop-out. A Socratic method of explanation compliments the commonsense approach of behaviour therapy. The rationale of treatment is explained and any odd ideas the subject may have about behaviour therapy are examined so that they do not discourage him from agreeing to a programme which is otherwise acceptable. Any distressing physical symptoms are discussed in full and their psychophysiological basis is explained. This indicates not only that the therapist appreciates the subject's distress, but the more understanding the subject has of the nature of his symptoms, the less they will bother him and the less he will be troubled by fears of their possible consequences.

An explanation about treatment should cover several specific points:

1. Treatment is *client-directed*: nothing is done without prior negotiation, no surprises are sprung upon the unsuspecting subject and his agreement is sought before any potentially distressing procedure is introduced. The therapist should always be prepared to take the same risks as those expected of a client.
2. Most progress will be made *between* treatment sessions, during which time the subject is expected to complete, regularly and frequently, agreed 'homework' tasks. These may be time consuming, so the subject's application is essential and other activities may have to be relegated in importance at least until treatment is completed.
3. It is likely, although not essential for treatment to be effective, that programmes involving exposure to feared situations will evoke discomfort. However, this discomfort will decline, or habituate, if exposure is sufficiently prolonged. For the subject's benefit, habituation can be demonstrated either by devising an anxiety-provoking situation during the interview or by pointing out the way in which the subject's interview-related anxiety has declined since the start of the session.
4. Tasks are tackled in a gradual fashion so that initial success with easier tasks restores confidence for more difficult ones. A formal hierarchy may be used but is not essential. Tasks should be repeatable and, as well as being components of treatment, it is ideal if they involve an additional pay-off for the subject.
5. Treatment is usually time limited. Progress is reassessed after an agreed number of sessions to decide whether further contact is likely to be worth while.
6. A friend or relative may be recruited and 'trained' to act as a co-therapist because it is unlikely that the therapist will be able to afford sufficient time to supervise all sessions.
7. Before treatment begins, specific *therapeutic targets* are established for each problem. Targets should be:
    (a) precisely described in behavioural terms;
    (b) realistic;
    (c) relevant to the problem and representative of progress;
    (d) morally and legally acceptable;
    (e) desirable for the subject.

Recreating the subject's problem and symptoms during the assessment session is a great help towards deciding whether behavioural methods will be both suitable and acceptable. The height phobic, for example, may be asked to climb as far as he can up a fire-escape. This simple manoeuvre, called a *behavioural test*, not only leaves the subject in no doubt as to what may be expected of him or her in treatment, but it provides an unambiguous behavioural measure of the severity of the problem and indicates the level at which treatment must begin. It is also a convenient moment to test whether behavioural methods are likely to prove effective. The therapist uses prompting, praise and modelling to persuade the subject to improve upon performance. The longer the subject tolerates the situation, the more likely his or her symptoms are to habituate and the more progress he or she will make. Performance here is a good indicator of how cooperative he or she will be in treatment and the therapist is given an opportunity to identify and discuss the subject's current coping strategies and any irrational ideas which might be maintaining his or her symptoms unnecessarily. It is, of course, a first step in treatment and, if it is carried out properly, *a test of behaviour therapy* leaves the subject with a sense of achievement from the first contact.

Measurement and record keeping

Behaviour therapists like their subjects to measure items such as symptom severity, problem severity and the degree of handicap in key areas of life. Measures applied before and after treatment and at follow-up indicate treatment progress, overall effectiveness and the durability of treatment. The ease of measurement has not only made efficacy studies possible, but it has important clinical implications, because the subject discovers that limits can now be applied to a symptom or problem which previously seemed to be boundless.

Standard questionnaires are available for some items but, for a symptom such as anxiety, a simple, visual analogue scale is quite sufficient. Its range is a matter of personal preference. Some therapists like to use a 0 to 8 scale and others prefer 0 to 100. In either case, 0 represents the total absence of the symptom and the top of the scale represents the most severe the symptom has ever been. Somewhere between the two is a level at which the symptom becomes tolerable. It may be useful to incorporate this level into treatment targets. With a little instruction on the use of these scales, most subjects achieve a level of reliability from which treatment progress can be assessed.

Behaviour therapists also like their subjects to keep records in the form of a *daily diary*. This would contain information about task completion and associated symptom severity. A diary is also useful for getting at the cognitive components of a problem, because relevant details can be recorded as they occur. As well as providing information for the subject and therapist to process at their next meeting, the need to produce a diary encourages work on task assignments. The effort which has gone into producing a diary is also a good indicator of motivation in cases of doubt.

Factors influencing suitability for treatment

In the individual case, suitability for treatment depends upon certain features of the problem and upon factors in the client. The problem should be:

1. Current.
2. Predictable.
3. Repetitive.
4. Describable in behavioural terms.
6. Sufficiently disabling to warrant the necessary therapeutic investment.

The client should:

1. Understand and accept treatment.
2. Not exhibit any psychiatric disorder which would contraindicate the use of behaviour therapy. No contraindications are absolute but four are important
   (a) severe depression;
   (b) some forms of organic brain damage;
   (c) active psychosis;
   (d) a disorder of personality which results in the subject's inability to stick to a structured treatment programme.

The diagnosis alone is a reliable guide as to whether or not a problem is likely to be suitable for behaviour therapy. For some conditions, behaviour therapy is the treatment of choice. These are:

- Simple phobias.
- Social anxiety and social skills dysfunction.
- Agoraphobia.
- Obsessive–compulsive rituals.
- Psychosexual dysfunction.
- Some childhood disorders such as school refusal.

There are many other conditions in which behaviour therapy has a role, though not necessarily as the treatment of choice. This list is not exhaustive.

- Depression.
- Alcoholism.
- Drug abuse.
- Smoking.
- Appetitive disorders.
- Habit disorders and tics.
- Hypochondriasis.
- Obsessional thoughts and ruminations.
- Grief reactions.
- Anxiety states.
- Marital dysfunction.
- Child abuse.
- Compulsive gambling.
- Some childhood disorders.

Working out a treatment package

The range of techniques which is available usually means that more than one approach can be offered to treat any given problem. In many cases, a package consisting of various techniques is used. The therapist may present the full range of techniques to the subject, cafeteria-style, with advice about the implications of each. The subject may be given the choice of those which he thinks will suit him best, though it must be said that the therapist does guide the choice and would strongly advise a technique if it was particularly indicated for a specific problem.

As treatment progresses, the focus of therapy may switch from one problem to another. This is not unreasonable and behaviour therapy is flexible enough to accommodate such changes. However, the experienced therapist is always alert to the subject whose attention shifts from problem to problem so frequently that it is impossible to do much effective work upon any of them.

Efficacy, limitations and therapeutic failures

The disorders in which behaviour therapy may be usefully employed account for one in eight of psychiatric outpatient referrals. The effectiveness of behaviour therapy has been demonstrated in a number of controlled trials and single-case studies, but it has its critics. For example, because behaviour therapy is oriented towards the relief of symptoms, it has been suggested that its failure to deal with any underlying neurotic conflict might result in the emergence of fresh symptoms, a phenomenon known as *symptom substitution*. In fact, what evidence there is suggests that this occurs rarely, if at all. Furthermore, treatment gains appear not only to be maintained in the long run, but there is a progressive improvement in various areas of life following behaviour therapy.

Behavioural programmes are, however, not always successful. There are several reasons for this, some of which are avoidable. The most common, perhaps, is a subject's failure to comply with the agreed treatment programme. This may be because treatment tasks are too difficult or because coexisting life stresses are interfering with therapy. Some subjects are discouraged by counter-instructions from friends, neighbours or family. Obsessional subjects may use mental 'tricks' (*internal avoidance*) to 'make good' the omission of a ritual. Where exposure methods are used, too short an exposure session is not only ineffective but may even make the problem worse and there is a very small group of subjects whose anxiety fails to habituate even with prolonged exposure. Occasionally, the problem has been misidentified, with the result that treatment targets are wrong. Finally, there may be a coexisting psychiatric disorder such as depression. Severe depression interferes with between-session improvements, even when there is good

progress within treatment sessions. It must be treated before lasting therapeutic gains can be made.

Behaviour Therapy in Institutions

The skills which are required for independent living are frequently deficient
in the behavioural repertoire of subjects who are cared for in the institutions
for the chronically mentally disordered. In mental handicap these skills may
never have been acquired and in chronic mental illness, particularly in
chronic schizophrenia, skills may have been lost due to the ravages of the
primary disorder or as a result of prolonged institutionalisation. In some
cases, aggressive, destructive and bizarre behaviours have taken their place.
The aims of treatment are:

1. To improve the quality of life of the subject.
2. To establish the skills necessary for life in the community.
3. To eliminate unwanted behaviours that constitute major management
   problems.

The methods used are based upon the principles of *operant conditioning*
which predict that behaviours are influenced by their consequences. Whenever possible, operant programmes emphasise the reinforcement of desirable
behaviours. Aversive methods are used only when positive reinforcement
and other methods of treatment have failed. The subject, his or her relatives
and the staff must be fully informed of the aims and methods of treatment
and the rights, privileges and standards of care of subjects should be
rigorously maintained.

According to the principles of operant conditioning, the reinforcer
should be delivered as soon as possible following the behaviour it is intended to reinforce. This is relatively simple where the therapist is working on a one-to-one basis with an individual. However, where few staff
supervise many subjects, the practical problems of selecting and delivering
the requisite reinforcer for each individual is overcome by the use of
tokens (*secondary reinforcers*) which are contingent upon the required
behaviour. Tokens may be exchanged later for goods and privileges (*primary
reinforcers*).

Such programmes, known as *token economies*, have been criticised on
academic and ethical grounds and the role of tokens as conditioned reinforcers has been questioned. Nevertheless, token economies do seem to be
useful for producing desirable behavioural changes in subjects and, perhaps,
in the staff who supervise them.

Commonly used Behavioural Techniques

Methods of increasing desirable behaviours

An event which increases the likelihood that a behaviour will recur is a reinforcer. *Positive reinforcement* involves the addition of something that is equivalent to a reward and *negative reinforcement* involves the removal of something that is aversive. Each increases the likelihood of recurrence of any behaviour upon which it is contingent. Sweets are useful as reinforcers for children, and tobacco, money and privileges for adults. The nature of the reinforcer depends upon the likes and dislikes of the individual and in all cases it is gradually replaced by social reinforcement as targets are achieved.

In *shaping*, behaviours are achieved by reinforcing small steps or approximations towards the final response. *Chaining* involves the sequential linking of the component responses which constitute an organised behaviour with reinforcement being contingent only upon the final response in the chain. Chaining is often most easily carried out in reverse, beginning with the terminal response and progressively building up prior behaviours. Responses can be initiated by verbal or physical *prompting* or by *modelling* in which the therapist demonstrates the required behaviour to the subject. *Fading* involves gradually withdrawing prompts, as the behaviour is achieved.

These simple procedures have been applied with success to a range of human behaviours. Although operant methods are usually associated with the management of problems in institutions, it will be clear that the principles of reinforcement are equally fundamental to the treatment of neurotic disorders. Indeed in some, such as certain forms of marital therapy, an operant approach may be the central feature of treatment.

Methods of reducing undesirable behaviours

Aversive techniques, which employ noxious stimuli to eliminate unwanted behaviours, were once used extensively in the management of sexual deviations, alcoholism, drug abuse and certain specific behaviours such as self-mutilation, which are seen in institutions. Electric shocks and chemically induced nausea were commonly used as aversive stimuli but the methods lost popularity partly because results were rather disappointing. In some instances, particularly with the mentally handicapped, aversive stimuli can paradoxically reinforce the undesirable behaviour.

Removing the subject from all reinforcers, called 'time out', is a form of *extinction* procedure in which unwanted behaviours gradually disappear because they are no longer reinforced. The use of aversive stimuli in imagination is called *covert sensitisation* and has been used particularly in the management of deviant sexual behaviours and urges. It involves the client imagining himself performing the deviant act and this is interrupted by an aversive scene, such as the approach of a policeman to arrest him for his behaviour.

The therapeutic component of the behavioural management of obsessive–compulsive rituals is called *response prevention*. It consists of preventing the subject from indulging in a ritual until the urge to do so has passed. Teaching a subject to interrupt intrusive, obsessional thoughts by shouting 'stop' is called *thought stopping*. The subject then learns to internalise the order so that he or she can use the technique in any situation. Tics and habit disorders are managed by instructing the subject to follow the unwanted behaviour with one which is incompatible with it, a method known as *habit reversal*. Alternatively, the subject may be instructed to practise the unwanted behaviour until he or she tires of it. This is *satiation* or *massed practice*.

Self-observation, a feature of all *self-control* methods, can reduce the frequency of unwanted behaviours, such as cigarette smoking, by itself. It may be combined with *self-reinforcement*, where the subject rewards him- or herself for periods of desirable behaviour, or *self-punishment* for failure to achieve an agreed target. A financial penalty is called a *response cost*. Reducing the opportunity for a behaviour by manipulating the conditions under which it occurs is known as *stimulus control* and has been used to treat appetitive disorders and alcohol abuse.

Methods of reducing anxiety and fear

Exposure to feared situations can be carried out slowly or rapidly. *Slow exposure, desensitisation*, involves inducing a state of relaxation before a feared stimulus is introduced. Anxiety is minimised by choosing stimuli from a hierarchy of cues of increasing difficulty, hence the term '*systematic desensitisation*', and by interrupting exposure as soon as the subject indicates arousal. The stimulus is reintroduced only when a state of relaxation has been re-established. It is supposed to work by weakening the fear-evoking property of the stimulus by presenting it only during relaxation – a state that is incompatible with fear. This principle is known as reciprocal inhibition. It is a slow, tedious method which has been largely superseded by *rapid exposure*. Here, anxiety is permitted but exposure is prolonged so that *habituation* occurs. When carried out in vivo it is sometimes called *flooding* and its use in imagination, at which time maximal anxiety levels are evoked, is called *implosion*. Exposure is useful whenever there is avoidance of feared situations. Its effect is impaired by depression and by excessive use of alcohol and tranquillisers.

Relaxation therapy can take several forms though none seems to be more effective than another. Methods commonly involve progressive muscular relaxation or mental imagery. Taped instructions are useful and it is usual to link the relaxed state with a pleasant, imagined scene so that relaxation can be induced in any situation merely by recalling the scene.

Biofeedback consists of providing the subject with information about the state of his or her physiological functioning. One of the physiological accompaniments of anxiety, such as heart rate, galvanic skin response (GSR) or electromyogram (EMG) is converted, electronically, into a visual or auditory signal. The subject learns to alter the signal and so his or her state of arousal. It has been used to treat generalised tension and anxiety. Migraine, tension headaches and other muscular dysfunctions may also respond.

Methods of altering social behaviours

Difficulties in forming and sustaining relationships with others are commonly associated with psychiatric disorders. *Social skills training* aims to modify a subject's social behaviour in order to help him or her to overcome these difficulties. There is some evidence that social skills training produces an improvement in overall psychological adjustment as well as in social competence.

Treatment usually involves a programmed course which is applied to a group of selected subjects. Behaviours are modelled by the therapist and the group follows this with role-play and rehearsal under controlled conditions. The therapist's role is to guide, coach and encourage the group. Group members offer feedback with an initial emphasis upon successful aspects of performance. Shortcomings are examined later. Closed-circuit television and video play-back can be invaluable during feedback. Social interactions are examined in terms of separate components such as eye contact, posture, speaking skills etc. This makes the role-play more manageable for the group and it helps to structure feedback. Exercises increase in complexity as skills develop.

Summary

Behaviour therapy is an empirically derived form of psychological treatment whose effectiveness has been demonstrated in a range of human disorders. It is distinguished by a characteristic symptom-oriented approach and by its emphasis upon the current determinants of the clinical problem rather than its historical antecedents. Treatment is often a matter of commonsense and follows logically from an accurate functional analysis.

The treatment of neurotic disorders is a collaborative process in which the subject directs his or her own treatment with guidance from the therapist. The subject is responsible for completing negotiated task assignments and for maintaining a daily record from which treatment progress can be assessed. In most cases a flexible, multi-technique approach is used.

Further Reading

COBB, J., McDONALD, R., MARKS, I. et al. (1980). Marital versus exposure therapy: psychological treatments of co-existing marital and phobic-obsessive problems. *Behaviour and Modification* 4, 3–16.

LIBERMAN, R.P. (1972). *A Guide to Behavioural Analysis and Therapy*. New York: Pergamon.

MARKS, I.M. (1978). *Living with Fear*. New York: McGraw-Hill.

MUNBY, M. and JOHNSTON, D.W. (1980). Agoraphobia: the long-term follow-up of behavioural treatment. *British Journal of Psychiatry* 137, 418–427.

STERN, R.S. (1978). *Behavioural Techniques*. London: Academic Press.

Chapter 10
Cognitive Therapy

DAVID M. CLARK

'Can you keep from crying by considering?', said Alice.
'That's the way it's done', the Queen said.
From *Alice Through the Looking Glass* by Lewis Carroll (1872)

Cognitive therapy is a relatively recent form of psychotherapy which aims to alleviate emotional problems by helping individuals to identify and change faulty patterns of thinking. It is based on a cognitive model of emotional disorders (Beck, 1976). The central notion in this model is the idea that it is not events per se but rather peoples' interpretations of events which is responsible for the production of negative emotions such as anxiety, anger or depression. The interpretations considered important in depression relate to perceived loss of a relationship, status or efficacy. In anxiety the important interpretations, or cognitions, relate to perceived danger of such a loss or of damage, sickness or death. Clearly, there are numerous occasions on which individuals experience genuine loss or are in objectively dangerous situations. Furthermore, many cases of anxiety and depression are triggered by adverse life events. However, cognitive theorists claim that, in pathological mood states, thinking is unrealistic in the sense that it involves an overestimate of the loss or danger inherent in the persons' situations, and that it is this distorted pattern of thinking which helps to maintain emotional disorders.

Reciprocal Relationship between Thinking, Emotion and Behaviour

The cognitive model of emotional disorders assumes that there are a series of reciprocal relationships between thinking and behaviour and between thinking and emotion. Examples of some of these reciprocal relationships, which play a key role in maintaining emotional states, are given below.

1. Recent work on the effects of mood on memory (Bower, 1981; Teasdale, 1983) indicates that depressed mood facilitates the retrieval from memory of negative information and impairs retrieval of positive information. When taken in conjunction with the suggestion that certain types of negative thoughts produce depressed mood, this work indicates that a depressed person is trapped in a vicious circle in which negative thinking produces depressed mood and then depressed mood increases the probability of those negative thoughts which are likely to cause a further increase in depression, so perpetuating the disorder.

2. A second vicious cycle also exists in depression. Believing that they are ineffective and likely to fail, depressed people often withdraw from everyday activities. This means that they are unlikely to experience any positive events which might contradict their negative view of themselves and hence alleviate their depression.

3. In anxiety, two further sets of vicious circles exist. First, once a person sees the situation as dangerous, he or she selectively attends to information which might strengthen the perception of danger. For example, a speaker who is anxious might look round the audience, notice that there are a few people at the back who seem to be going to sleep, and then think, 'they have already decided the talk is useless, and everyone else is going to start nodding off soon. I'm boring them'. Secondly, the symptoms of anxiety are often interpreted as further sources of danger producing a further vicious circle which tends to maintain or exacerbate an anxiety reaction. For example, blushing may be taken as an indication that one has made a fool of oneself leading to further embarrassment and blushing; a shaking hand may be taken as an indication of impending loss of control leading to more anxiety and shaking; or a racing heart may be taken as evidence of an impending heart attack producing further anxiety and cardiac symptoms.

The reciprocal relationship between perceived danger and symptoms of anxiety plays a particularly important role in patients who suffer from panic attacks. A panic attack consists of a sudden onset, intense feeling of apprehension or impending doom associated with a range of physical sensations. Cognitive theories of panic (Beck et al., 1985; Clark, 1986) propose that such attacks are caused by the misinterpretation of normal bodily sensations as indications of an impending physical or mental catastrophe (for example, perceiving palpitations as evidence of an impending heart attack, or perceiving unusual and racing thoughts as evidence that one is about to go mad).

The particular sequence of events that it has been suggested occurs in a panic attack is shown in Figure 10.1. A wide range of stimuli appear to provoke attacks. These can be external (such as a supermarket for an agoraphobic) but more often are internal (a bodily sensation or mental image). If these stimuli are perceived as a sign of danger, a state of

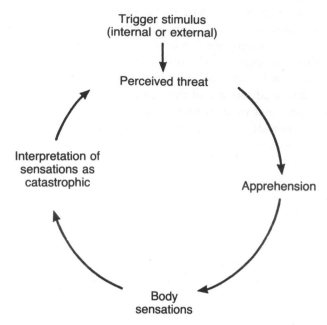

Figure 10.1 The suggested sequence of events in a panic attack. (Reproduced from D. M. Clark (1986), with permission of Pergamon Press.)

apprehension results. This state is associated with a wide range of bodily sensations. If these anxiety-produced sensations are interpreted in a catastrophic fashion, a further increase in apprehension occurs. This then produces a further increase in bodily sensations, leading to a vicious circle which culminates in a panic attack.

Features of Cognitive Therapy

The suggestion that emotional disorders are maintained by unrealistic thinking leads naturally to the idea that emotional problems can be treated by teaching people how to identify, evaluate and change their distorted thoughts and associated behaviours. A variety of cognitive and behavioural techniques are used to achieve this aim. Behavioural techniques play an important part in therapy because certain types of behaviour (such as avoidance) help to maintain distorted beliefs. Also, one of the most effective ways of modifying beliefs is to test them out in real life.

Cognitive therapy is a relatively brief and time-limited treatment (between 5 and 25 weekly sessions) which aims to teach patients a series of skills that they can use not only to overcome their current difficulties, but also to deal with future emotional problems and setbacks. Therapy sessions are highly structured. They start by setting an agenda, which lists items to be dealt with during the session. Patient and therapist agree the contents of the agenda. This usually includes a review of the previous week's homework and then covers one or two specific problems which will be the main focus of the session. Within the session, frequent feedback is used to guarantee mutual understanding and the session ends with a homework assignment which follows up the topic discussed during the session.

At the start of treatment, therapists aim to demonstrate the connection between thoughts and feelings. This can be done by reviewing examples from the patients' own experience and also by discussing hypothetical situations, e.g. imagining how you would feel if you are at home one night, heard a crash in another room, and then thought 'there is a burglar in the room', or instead thought 'the window was left open and the wind has blown something over'.

Next, patients are trained to identify anxiety- or depression-related cognitions. Sometimes these are images, rather than thoughts, and initially can be difficult to identify, partly because they are very brief and come to mind automatically. Once identified, attempts are made to modify the thoughts. Although therapists may be convinced of the irrationality of their patients' thoughts, they should not 'lecture' a patient. Instead, therapy is a collaborative exercise similar to that of a scientific team. The patient's thoughts are treated as hypotheses, with therapist and patient together collecting data to determine whether the hypotheses are accurate or helpful. The two main sources of data are discussion and behavioural experiments.

Verbal challenging of negative thoughts

A daily record of dysfunctional thoughts is shown in Table 10.1. This sheet is used to record and evaluate negative thoughts. Several illustrations of such thoughts and patients' responses to them are given in the table. Within treatment sessions, the therapist asks a series of questions which are aimed at helping patients to identify rational answers to their negative thoughts. Between sessions, patients attempt to put into practice the questioning skills they have learnt in sessions by recording and challenging negative thoughts as they arise. Examples of some of the questions which are particularly useful in helping patients to identify answers to their negative thoughts are: 'What evidence do I have for this thought?', 'Is there an alternative way of looking at the situation?', 'How would someone else think in my situation?', 'Am I setting myself an unrealistic or unobtainable standard?', and 'Am I thinking in all-or-nothing terms?'. In general, therapists prefer not to answer negative thoughts themselves, but instead ask questions that help patients to produce their own answers to their negative thoughts. This 'Socratic' style is used because research in social psychology suggests that people are more likely to believe information that contradicts their belief if they produce it themselves.

Table 10.1 A daily record of dysfunctional thoughts

Situation Describe: 1. Actual event leading to unpleasant emotion, or 2. Stream of thoughts, daydream, or recollection, leading to unpleasant emotion	Emotion(s) 1. Specify sad/anxious/angry etc. 2. Rate degree of emotion, 1–100	Automatic thought(s) 1. Write automatic thought(s) that preceded emotion(s) 2. Rate belief in automatic thought(s) 0–100%	Rational response 1. Write rational response to automatic thought(s) 2. Rate belief in rational response, 0–100%	Outcome 1. Re-rate belief in automatic thought(s) 0–100% 2. Specify and rate subsequent emotions, 0–100	Further action
Attending a social function at my husband's work. Don't know how many people and most of them know each other. Not being included in the conversation.	Anxious 70	I am boring tonight	There are lots of explanations for people having difficulty talking to a stranger other than finding them boring. Also I'm not evaluating other people so why should they be evaluating me	1. 10% 2. Anx. 0	Next time: 1. Give the other people some 'free information' about me to help them include me in their conversation 2. Ask them about themselves 3. Stop mind reading
		That means I am a boring person	If I am boring tonight that doesn't mean I'm always boring. Anyway nobody is boring through and through		
		Everyone hates a boring person therefore nobody will like me	You don't have to be the life and soul of a party to be liked. Many 'quiet' people are liked and loved by others		
In supermarket, suddenly felt faint, hot and breathless	Panic 90	I'm going to collapse/faint 80%	Just because I feel faint it doesn't mean to say I will faint. I've never fainted before when anxious. Furthermore you need a blood pressure drop to faint and blood pressure is up in anxiety so I'm less likely to faint than if calm. I feel faint because of overbreathing and blood going to muscles. Both normal responses. 95%	1. 10% 2. Panic 10	Next time as soon as I feel faint, rehearse answers to my thoughts, control breathing and maybe take pulse to check BP is not down

Behavioural experiments

In addition to discussing the evidence for and against negative beliefs, cognitive therapists also encourage patients to engage in behavioural experiments to test out their beliefs. An example of behavioural experiments is provided by the case of a housewife who experienced frequent panic attacks which were frightening because she believed they meant she had a serious cardiac condition. Negative medical tests and reassurance from her physician failed to modify this belief. However, reproduction of her feared symptoms by voluntary hyperventilation allowed her to entertain the idea that her symptoms might be partly due to stress-induced hyperventilation. Her objection that she noticed her heart beat most of the time, and that this must indicate that there was something wrong with her heart, was countered with the alternative suggestion that she noticed her heart more because of her fears, which led her to focus on her body. To test this suggestion, she was asked to close her eyes and concentrate on her heart. To her surprise she found that simply attending to her heart enabled her to detect her pulse throughout her body and reproduce her most alarming symptoms.

Assumption techniques

As well as dealing with specific thoughts that occur in particular situations, therapists also attempt to challenge general beliefs (dysfunctional assumptions), which may make an individual prone to becoming depressed or anxious in the first place. For example, a generally anxious patient who frequently has the thought, 'I will never get everything done', may be prone to this thought because of an extreme perfectionist belief such as 'I always have to do things properly'. One technique which could be used to challenge this belief would be discussion of its advantages and disadvantages. This discussion would reveal that the belief's advantages (it can sometimes produce very good work) are vastly outweighed by its disadvantages (it produces considerable anxiety which prevents you from doing your best; it makes you unwilling to take risks, unnecessarily restricting your range and preventing you from making the mistakes which are necessary for learning; it does not allow you to let mistakes be noticed by others and therefore prevents you from obtaining valuable feedback).

Effectiveness of Cognitive Therapy

Cognitive therapy is a relatively recent development in psychotherapy. So far controlled trials of the effectiveness of cognitive therapy have largely focused on its use as a treatment for depression and anxiety (see Clark, 1990, for a recent review). In depression, studies assessing immediate response to treatment indicate that cognitive therapy is at least as effective as tricyclic antidepressants and there is some evidence that cognitive therapy may be more effective at reducing relapse. In anxiety, cognitive therapy has been shown to be a highly effective treatment for social phobia, generalised anxiety disorder and panic disorder, with the immediate post-treatment results comparing favourably with those obtained with well-conducted behavioural treatment. Encouraged by cognitive therapy's success in depression and anxiety, research workers have recently developed promising cognitive approaches to the treatment of other problems such as personality disorders (Beck and Freeman, 1990) and somatic problems (Salkovskis, 1989). The results of controlled trials evaluating cognitive therapy's effectiveness in these areas are eagerly awaited.

References

BECK, A.T. (1976). *Cognitive Therapy and the Emotional Disorders*. New York: International University Press.

BECK, A.T., EMERY, G. and GREENBERG, R.L. (1985). *Anxiety Disorders and Phobias*. New York: Basic Books.

BECK, A.T. and FREEMAN, A. (1990). *Cognitive Therapy of Personality Disorders*. New York: Guilford.

BOWER, G. (1981). Mood and Memory. *American Psychologist* **36**, 129–148.

CLARK, D.M. (1986). A cognitive approach to panic. *Behaviour Research and Therapy* **24**, 461–470.

CLARK, D.M. (1990). Cognitive therapy for anxiety and depression; is it better than drug treatment in the long-term? In: K. Hawton and P. Cowen (Eds) *Dilemmas and Difficulties in the Management of Psychiatric Patients*. Oxford: Oxford University Press.

SALKOVSKIS, P.M. (1989). Somatic problems: In: K. Hawton, P. M. Salkovskis, J. Kirk and D. M. Clark (Eds), *Cognitive Behaviour Therapy for Psychiatric Problems: A Practical Guide*. Oxford: Oxford University Press.

TEASDALE, J.D. (1983). Negative thinking in depression: cause, effect or reciprocal relationship? *Advances in Behaviour Research and Therapy* **5**, 3–25.

Further Reading

The following books are recommended for readers interested in a more detailed description of how to do cognitive therapy.

BECK, A.T., RUSH, A.J. SHAW, B.F. and EMERY, G. (1979). *Cognitive Therapy of Depression*. New York: Guilford Press.

BURNS, D. (1980). *Feeling Good*. New York: New American Library.

HAWTON, K., SALKOVSKIS, P., KIRK, J. and CLARK, D. M. (1989). *Cognitive Behaviour Therapy for Psychiatric Problems: A Practical Guide*. Oxford: Oxford University Press.

SCOTT, J., WILLIAMS, J.M.G. and BECK, A.T. (1989). *Cognitive Therapy: A Clinical Casebook* London: Routledge.

Further General Reading

BLOCH, S. (1979). *An Introduction to the Psychotherapies*. Oxford: Oxford University Press.

BROWN, D. and PEDDER, J. (1979). *Introduction to Psychotherapy*. London: Tavistock Publications.

LOMAS, P. (1973). *True and False Experience*. London: Alan Lane.

RIPPERE, V. and WILLIAMS R. (1985). *The Wounded Healer*. Chichester: Wiley.

STORR, A. (1979). *The Art of Psychotherapy*. London: Secker and Warburg, Heinemann Medical.

Index

abreaction, 21
acting out, 67
addictions, 5
Adler, Alfred, 40, 41, 93
advice and guidance, 3
age of patient, 6
agoraphobia, 143
alcohol,
    abuse, 46, 67, 96, 135, 138, 139
        by medical staff, 50
    use, 131
allergies, 103
alliance, therapeutic, 30–31
alter-ego, 44
ambivalence, 5
anger, of seriously ill patients, 64–65
'Animus'/'Anima', 40
Anna O, 15
anorexia, family effects, 108, 109, 111, 112
antecedents, 131–132
anti-racist training, 120–122
antidepressants, 36
anxiety, 5, 6, 22–23, 142 148, 143, 145, 147
    internal, 7
    in physical illness, 61–62
    reduction, 139–140
    social, 135
    states, 25, 135
appetitive disorders, 56, 135, 139
    see also anorexia
archetype, 41
assessment,
    in behaviour therapy, 130–132
    for group therapy, 101–103
    psychiatric, 130–132
    of suicide patients, 72
association, free, 31, 43
Association for Family Therapy, 127
assumption techniques, 145–146
asthma, 5, 25, 32, 84, 103, 110
attachment behaviour, 41

attention, selective, 17
aversive techniques, 138
avoidance, 132
    internal, 136
    phobic, 8

back pain, psychologically caused, 85–86
balance, in a group, 96
Balint, Michael and Enid, 2, 50, 78–82
Bateson, Gregory, 95, 101
behaviour,
    antisocial, 25, 137
    desirable, encouragement of, 138
    factors influencing, 17–21
    maladapted, 132
    modification, 3, 138–140
    non-verbal, 31
    relation to emotion and thinking, 142–144
    undesirable, 4
        control of, 67
        reduction of, 138–140
behaviour therapist, directive style, 130
behaviour therapy, 36, 129–140
    contraindications, 135
    duration, 129–130, 133
    empirical nature, 129
    in institutions, 137
    limitations, 136
    measurement in, 134
    preparation for, 132–134
    suitability of, 134–135
    techniques, 138–140
    treatment package, 136
behavioural,
    analysis, 131
    approach, to symptoms, 129
    disorders, 124
    techniques, 57
    test, 133–134
behaviourists, 13
bereavement, 5, 125

151

Berne, Eric, 17, 42
biofeedback, 140
Bion, W., 93
biopsychosocial model, 56
body,
    image disturbance, 60
    and mind, 83–86
borderline patients, 46
brain damage, 135
Breuer, Josef, 15
British Association of Psychotherapists, 1
British Psychoanalytical Society, 1

cancer, 68, 103
    breast, 64
    cervical, 62
    psychological reactions to, 59
casualty departments, suicidal patients in, 70–73
catharsis, 21
Centre for Family Studies, Milan, 119
cerebral states, organic, 56
chaining, 138
challenging, of negative thoughts, 145–146
change, in family, 112, 116–119
Charcot, Dr, 15
chemotherapy, 60
child,
    abuse, 135
    development, 106–107
clarification, 32
clinical indications, for psychotherapy, 5–7
co-therapist,
    in behaviour therapy, 133
    in group therapy, 97
cognitive therapy, 142–148
    duration, 144
    effectiveness, 147–148
    features of, 144–148
colostomy, 60
communication via symptoms, 101
community, therapeutic, 95
conductor, of a group, 94
conflict, importance of, 43
confrontation, 3, 32
confusion state, 9
conscious, 17–18
consequences, of maladaptive behaviour, 132
content, latent and manifest, 32
contract, doctor–patient, 26
control,
    over illness, 59
    of unacceptable behaviour, 67
coping, 66
    with illness, 59, 64, 65
    mechanisms,
        doctors', 50
        patients', 25
counselling, 82
    non-medical, 4
countertransference, 9, 29–30
criminality, 67

crisis management, 4, 5, 103
curative factors, in group therapy, 100
cybernetics, 109

death,
    approach of, 60
    preparation for, 54, 58
    talking about, 52
defences, 4
    against physical illness, 60, 62–63
    ego, 22–23
    of medical students, 49
    respect for, 26
    types of, 7
degenerative disorders, psychological reactions
        to, 59, 65
denial, 8, 24, 72
    of physical illness, 62–64
dependence, of ill patients, 66
depression, 5, 6, 25, 142–148, 143, 145, 147
    in physical illness, 61–62
    severe, contraindicates behaviour therapy,
        135, 136
desensitisation, 139
destructive acts, 67
diabetics, labile, 112, 113
diagnosis,
    empathic, 3
    in general practice, 76–77
diary, daily, 134, 145–146
displacement, 8, 24, 68
distortions, in relationships, 7
divorce, 5
doctor,
    apostolic function, 81–82
    coping mechanisms, 50
    defence mechanisms, 25, 50
    emotions and feelings, 25, 48
    importance of personal therapy for, 3, 5,
        99
    temptations for, 28
doctor–patient relationship, 1, 2, 30, 35, 50, 75,
        85, 88
dreams, 10, 19
drug,
    abuse, 46, 67, 96, 124, 135, 138
        by medical profession, 50
    doctor, 82
    overdoses, 70
    therapy, 2, 36, 57, 62, 126
Durkheim, E, 92
dysmenorrhoea, 76, 84, 103

education,
    medical, 48
    use of group approaches in, 103
ego, 18–19, 40
    analysts, 42
    defence mechanisms, 22–23
    states, 17, 42
    strength, of patient, 6

emotion,
    expressed, 86, 113
    thinking and behaviour, 142–144
emotional,
    experience, corrective, 45
    problems, of hospital patients, 55
empathy, in analysis, 45
encounter groups, 95
epilepsy, 59
eros, 19
escape behaviour, 132
ethnicity, impact of, 120–124
examination, of patients, 48
existential conditions, 5
expectations, unrealistic, 35
exposure, to feared situations, 139–140
extinction, 138
extroversion/intraversion, 40–41

facilitation, 3
fading, 138
family,
    boundaries, 109
    change, 112
    dance, 110, 116–119
    doctor see general practitioner
    effect of physical illness on, 58, 63
    extended, 125
    homeostasis, 109
    interactional model, 107–108
    involvement, 65, 67
    nuclear, 125
    organisation and interaction, 108–109
    patterns, 110
    problems, 100
    psychosomatic, 112
    remarried, 125
    schizophrenic, 112, 113, 124
    sharing feelings with, 62
    single-parent, 125, 126
    stability, 111–112, 116–119
    structures, 124–126
    subsystems and suprasystems, 109
Family Institute, 127
family therapists, 95
    further training, 127–128
family therapy, 41, 82, 101, 105–128
    controlled trials, 113
    examples, 113–119
    impact of race, ethnicity and social
        disadvantage, 120–124
    methods, 119–120
    role of practitioner, 126–127
    suitability for, 124
    what it is, 106–107
fear, reduction, 139–140
feelings, discussing and sharing, 61–62
Ferenczi, S., 44, 45
fighting spirit, 65
flash, interviews, 81
flooding, 139

Foulkes, S.H., 93–95
Frankfurt Institute for Social Research, 94
free association, 16
Freud, Sigmund, 7, 13–16, 27, 40
frustration, tolerance of, 6, 30
functional analysis, 131

gain, primary and secondary, 6, 33
gambling, compulsive, 135
gastrointestinal symptoms, 5, 25, 84
general practice,
    integration in, 80, 83
    psychotherapy in, 74–90
    time constraints, 88–90
general practitioner,
    access to, 77–78
    approach to psychotherapy, 74–90
    training of, 78–80
getting it off one's chest, 61
grandparents, 125
grief reactions, 35, 135
group therapist, training of, 99–101
group therapy, 92–103, 120–121
    history of, 92–96
    how it works, 99–101
    in the NHS, 95–96
    process, 98
    suitable patients, 101–103
    wider application, 103
groups,
    frequency and duration, 96
    in GP training, 79–80
    membership, 96
    open and closed, 97
guidelines,
    for choice of therapy, 34
    for group therapy referral, 101
guilt, medical students', 52–53

habit,
    disorders, 135, 139
    reversal, 139
habituation, 139
headaches,
    sexual, 100
    tension, 140
history,
    clinical, 57
    of group therapy, 92–96
    of psychotherapy, 12–17
holistic medicine, 56
homework,
    in behaviour therapy, 133
    in cognitive therapy, 145
hope, 3
hypertension, 25, 84
hypnosis, 15
hypochondria, 135
hysterical conversion states, 56

id, 18
identification, projective, 10

illness,
    abnormal behaviour in, 56
    causes and consequences, 56
    chronic, 58
    outcome, 60
    physical,
        anxiety and depression in, 61–62
        denial of, 62–64
        effect on family, 58
        emotional support in, 58
        priority in doctor's thought, 84
        psychiatric treatment in, 55
        psychological reactions to, 56, 58–61, 59, 84
    terminal,
        doctor's reaction to, 25, 28
        effect on family, 125
        psychological reactions to, 59
implosion, 139
incidence, of emotional or psychiatric disorders,
    75–76
independence, of ill patients, 66
individuation, 40
inferiority complex, 41
insight, 3, 21, 35, 45
Institute of Family Therapy, 127
Institute of Group Analysis, 99
institutional patients, 130, 137
integration, 5, 45
    in general practice, 80, 83
intelligence, of patient, 6
interpretation, 3, 32, 115–116
interview,
    flash, 81
    initial, 3
    psychotherapeutically oriented, 57

Jung, Carl C., 40

Klein, Melanie, 41–42
Kleinian school, 10, 29, 45
Kohut, H., 43–44, 45

Lewin, Kurt, 93, 95
liaison psychiatry, 55–73
libido, 20
life events, adverse, 142–148
listening, importance of, 33–34, 51, 75, 79, 88

marital problems, 135
Marx, Karl, 92
Marlborough Family Service, 120, 123
massed practice, 139
mastectomy, 60, 69
maternal behaviour, 106
measurement, in behaviour therapy, 134
medical, thinking, 84
medical students,
    anxiety, 25
    emotions and feelings, 48, 50
    guilt, 52–53
    phantasies, 48, 51

medical students (contd)
    reponsibilities, 102
    role, 51
memory, effect of mood, 143
migraine, 5, 25, 76, 84, 140
mistrust, of family therapist, 123, 124
modelling, 138
mood,
    depressed, 143
    effect on memory, 143
Moreno, J.L., 21, 93, 94
motivation, of patient, 6, 35, 103
motivation, unconscious, 17
musculoskeletal diseases, 5, 140
myocardial infarction, psychological reactions,
    59

narcissism, 46
neurosis, 35, 124, 130
non-family systems, 124–126
non-specific factors, 37
non-verbal behaviour, 61
Northfield Military Hospital, 94, 95
nursing, importance of, 53–54

obsessions, 117, 135
Oedipus complex, 9, 20
operant conditioning, 137
opportunistic approach, 74
over-confiding, 67–68
over-involvement, 67–68

panic,
    attacks, 143, 147
    disorder, 148
paranoia, 24
parasuicide, and liaison psychiatry, 70–71
patterns, in family behaviour, 110–111
perception, subliminal, 17
Perls, Fritz, 95
permission, to discuss feelings, 61
perpetuating factors, 131
'Persona', 40
personality,
    disorders, 35, 46, 135
    of doctor, 2
phantasies, medical students', 48, 51
Philadelphia Child Guidance Clinic, 112
phobias, 8, 118–119, 133, 135
physical illness see illness, physical
placebo effect, of doctor, 2
positions, depressive and paranoid–schizoid, 42
posthypnotic suggestion, 10
preconscious, 17
pregnancy, reaction of father to, 84–85
presentation, of symptoms, 86–88
processes, primary and secondary, 18
projection, 8, 23–24, 53
    excessive, 42
promiscuity, 67
prompting, 138
psychiatrist, general, 2

psychiatry, liaison, 55–73
psychoanalysis,
    classical, 7–11, 13, 36, 45, 99
    non-classical, 40–46
psychoanalytical theory, of groups, 94
psychodrama, 21, 93, 94, 98
psychodynamic,
    awareness, 35
    model, 13
psychological-mindedness, of patient, 6, 7, 35
psychological reactions, to physical illness,
    58–61
psychology,
    analytical, 40
    gestalt, 95
    individual, 41
    medical, 48
    of the self, 43, 44
psychosis, 34, 135
psychosocial, concepts, 16
psychosomatic, conditions, 5, 35
psychosis, 25
psychotherapist,
    personal integrity, 12
    registration, 1
    role in family therapy, 116
    training, 1, 2–3
psychotherapy,
    aims of, 21–22, 45–46
    clinical indications for, 5–7
    conduct of sessions, 3–4
    demands on patient, 35
    dynamic, 62
    in general practice, 74–90
    harmful effects, 12
    history and development, 12–17
    importance for therapists, 99
    individual, 2–3, 120–121
    insight-oriented, 4–5, 57, 66
    liaison, skills and techniques, 56–58
    neo-Freudian, 41
    schools of, 12
    setting for, 74
    skills and techniques, 31–34
    suitable patients for, 6–7, 34–36
    supportive, 3, 4, 5, 57, 61–62
    termination, 31
    types of practitioner, 1
    value of, 14
    see also behaviour therapy; cognitive therapy;
        family therapy

race, impact of, 120–124
rationalisation, 9
reaction formation, 9
reassurance, 3
record keeping, in behavioural therapy, 134
redundancy, 5
regression, 9, 99
reinforcement, in behaviour therapy, 137,
    138–140

relationships,
    personal, 74
    problems, 5, 22, 35, 41, 46, 100, 107, 124
    professional, 36
    social, 16, 92
    and suicide, 92
    therapeutic, 26–31
relaxation therapy, 139
renal failure, psychological reactions, 59
repression, 9, 23, 72
resistance, 31
response,
    cost, 139
    prevention, 139
retirement, 5, 116–119
ritualistic behaviour, 132
Rogers, Carl, 95
Royal College of General Practitioners, 82

satiation, 139
scapegoating, 24
schizoid patients, 46
schizophrenia, 5, 35, 137
    effect on family, 112, 113, 124
school refusal, 96, 135
self-awareness, 21
self-destructive acts, 70–71
self-determination, 42
self-esteem, 45
self-help groups, 68–69
self-observation, 139
self-poisoning, 56
self-psychology, 43–44
self-punishmsnt, 139
self-reinforcement, 139
sensitisation, covert, 138
separation–individuation, 41
setting, for therapy, 2, 74
sexual,
    instinct, 19
    problems, 5, 89–90, 96, 135, 138
    therapy, 82
sexuality, in medical examination, 49
'Shadow', 40
shaping, 138
silence, a problem, 4
slips, 'Freudian', 10, 18
smoking, 135
social,
    disadvantage, impact of, 120–124
    phobia, 148
    skills, 135, 140
Society for Analytical Psychotherapy, 1
sociocultural factors, 36
sociology, 92
somatisation, 24
splitting, 42
stability, family, 111–112, 116–119
staff training, group approaches in, 103
step-parents, 125
stimulus control, 139

sublimation, 9
suicide,
    acute management, 71–73
    Durkheim's study, 92
    fantasies, 72
    in medical profession, 50
    therapy after attempt, 73
super-ego, 18, 40
suppression, 9
Suttie, I.D., 44, 45
symptoms,
    amenability to psychological treatment, 103
    behavioural approach, 129
    as communication, 101
    presentation, 86–88
    substitution, 15, 16, 136
systems, approach, 41, 105, 108–109

T-groups, 93, 95
taboo on tenderness, 44
talking cure, 31, 36
targets, therapeutic, 133
Tavistock Clinic, 78–79
teamwork, 53
terminal illness see illness
termination, of psychotherapy, 31
thanatos, 19
therapeutic alliance, 30–31
therapeutic relationship, 26–31

therapy see cognitive therapy; family therapy;
    group therapy; psychotherapy
thinking, relation to emotion and behaviour,
    142–144
thought stopping, 139
thoughts, dysfunctional, 145–146
tics, 135, 139
time, in general practice, 88–90
time out, 138
token economies, 137
training,
    of family therapists, 127
    of general practitioners, 78–80
    of group psychotherapists, 99–101
    of medical students, 50
tranquillisers, use of, 131
transactional analysis, 17, 42
transference, 7, 9, 27–30, 43, 45
    modifications, 43–44
    positive and negative, 27
transposition, 99–100
trials, controlled, of family therapy,
    113
tuberculosis, 103

unconscious, 10, 17–18, 36
    personal and collective, 40

working through, 32–33, 99